Peril and Promise

Essays on Community in South Dakota and Beyond

Peril and Promise

*Essays on Community in
South Dakota and Beyond*

AASLH
"AWARD OF MERIT"
2008

Edited by Charles L. Woodard

Published by the South Dakota Agricultural Heritage Museum
A Department of South Dakota State University
925 11th Street, Brookings, SD 57007

Woodard, Charles L., Editor

ISBN: 13:978-0-615-16927-9

Printed in the United States of America by Edwards Brothers,
Ann Arbor, Michigan.

*Cover painting by Ted Kooser, two-term Poet Laureate of the United States
and winner of the 2005 Pulitzer Prize for Poetry.*

Acknowledgements

The South Dakota Humanities Council provided strong support as the idea for this book was developed, and as the book project evolved.

Additional much appreciated support was provided by South Dakota State University, by the community of Clear Lake, South Dakota, by the staff at the South Dakota Agricultural Heritage Museum, by the South Dakota State Historical Society, by the Rural Learning Center and Miner County Community Revitalization in Howard, South Dakota, and by photographers Richard Lee, Ruby Wilson, Eric Landwehr and John Miller. In addition, John Miller and Larry Rogers spent much time on the design of this book.

Contents

Introduction

Charles L. Woodard

Community. Say it out loud and the words "commune" and "unity" are resonant. Denotatively and connotatively, it is one of the most positive words in the language. Yet it is probably also one of our most loosely used words as well.

This book represents an extended and concerted effort to come to terms with the meaning of the word and to identify and argue for its most appropriate applications.

The book effort began with a conversation about community in an SDSU van returning from an academic conference about seven years ago. That conversation precipitated a gathering of a group of interested SDSU faculty members to discuss Robert Putnam's recently published book entitled *Bowling Alone: The Collapse and Revival of American Community.* Discussions continued, and eventually the members of what became known as "the community group" decided to assemble a collection of writings on what they had come to believe is a topic of strong and urgent importance to this state and region.

Early in the sequence, members of the group spent time in the community of Clear Lake, which was chosen because it is close enough to Brookings for easy access and yet far enough away to have some autonomy as a community. In interviews with Clear Lake residents and in program presentations to them, group members benefited from a variety of practical experiences with a specific community group and were so positively received that they were additionally motivated to continue the publication effort.

Another important motivation was the traditional idea of a university, an idea some of the group members have been discussing for a long time. The university, the community group clearly believes, is at its best an interdisciplinary and cross-cultural community of learners as well as teachers interactive with and responsive to other communities of its society and its world.

Then the writing process began. While the book was originally conceived of as simply a collection of essays, it evolved in the making of it, and eventually, discussion questions, photographs, an annotated bibliography and poems were added.

The discussion questions, the photographs and the annotated bibliography were added to make the book more useable in classrooms and in community discussion groups.

The poems were added because poetry is language intensified, an expression of the human heart and spirit which seems especially appropriate to the subject of this book. Placed where they are, in juxtaposition to essays which reflect and reiterate them or are in discussable contrast to them, the poems make the whole text a more complete community of expression.

The book is also sequenced to maximize its potential as an educational tool. The first essay is a foundational philosophical discussion of the idea of community, and the essays which follow it broaden the consideration of the topic to include additional reflection on the rural and the biological communities. These are followed by essays about what one contributor refers to as "communities of difference," that is, tribal communities past and present, tribal and non-tribal schools, and communities of writers. The final essays are mostly about recent and contemporary circumstances and experiences, including some specific proposals, from key disciplinary perspectives, for restoring and/or maintaining and/or enhancing community in this region.

Too often, changes occur because of indifference to them, and/or because of resignation, the belief that certain changes are inevitable no matter what anyone says or does. In contrast, a strong theme and argument throughout this book is that individuals and communities can successfully resist such thinking and the ways of being which are the consequences of it.

My friends and colleagues who are the authors of this book about community clearly believe that there is both peril and promise in the ideas about community and community change which have currency today. Their energetic and expressive writings are both highly informative and a challenge to their readers to be hopeful, and proactive in response to our region's urgent need for good community and good community development.

Many years ago, the Lakota chief Sitting Bull, a perceptive and visionary leader, offered an invitation and a challenge to which the authors of this book have responded thoughtfully and creatively. "Let us put our minds together," he said, "and see what future we can make for our children."

CLW

To Sally a fellow South Dakotan who understands something about Community John Miller

The Places We Treasure and Their Contribution to Our Lives

John E. Miller

Few things are more significant and important to us than the places we treasure. Think of Mark Twain's Hannibal, Franklin Roosevelt's Hyde Park, William Faulkner's Oxford, Laura Ingalls Wilder's "Little Town on the Prairie," Ansel Adams's Rocky Mountains, Willa Cather's Nebraska—the list could go on and on. The houses we inhabit, the neighborhoods we live in, the streets and sidewalks we navigate, and the natural environments we are blessed with all contribute in profound and mysterious ways to our moods and our morale. Cultural geographer Yi-Fu Tuan attached a name to the bond of affection that develops between people and a particular place, calling it "topophilia," that is, love of place.[1]

Few people exist apart from the community. Place and community are inextricably intertwined. Place helps to define community, and the residents of the community have a major say in what kinds of places they inhabit. They are active makers of the buildings, yards, streets, open spaces, parks, scenic vistas, gathering spots, community centers, and other places in which they live their lives. People who have no place to call home—transients, drifters, nomads—by the fact of their placelessness, exist outside of the community. We can learn much by thinking about the places that define our lives. "By the close study of a place, its people and character, its crops, products, paranoias, dialects, and failures, we come closer to our reality," writes novelist Louise Erdrich.[2]

However, space alone does not make a place. The latter carries with

5

it a welter of connotations and meanings that extend far beyond the specific physical characteristics attached to the former. A place emerges completely only when human beings pay careful attention to the space around them and make it their own, which usually entails physically modifying it in some fashion. Much of what we define as civilization is related to the myriad ways in which we think about, plan for, transform, and derive pleasure and meaning from our physical surroundings. In the process of transforming space into place, we enhance the quality and meaning of our lives.

Community also carries many meanings for most of us. Most commonly, we associate it with a group of people having common interests or sentiments and living in a particular area. While it is possible to think of widely dispersed groups of Cadillac drivers, E-mail users, or New York Yankee fans as communities, we generally expect a community to exist in a particular geographic location that brings its members together in face-to-face interaction. It was this sort of primary community that prevailed in the pre-modern era, before industrialism, urbanization, and technological advancement began to break down traditional patterns of behavior. The past century has witnessed a general loosening of ties connecting people and the substitution of more dispersed, amorphous, and contingent communities for the tightly knit ones that had tended to prevail earlier. Nevertheless, communities, by definition, link people together. "In its deepest sense," Thomas Bender writes, "a community is a communion."[3]

Alexis de Tocqueville, the celebrated French social observer, visited the United States during the 1830s and returned home to write what is generally thought to be the most perceptive account of American culture ever published. He considered the tendency to form associations and the vitality of community in the United States to be one of the country's major identifying features. "Americans of all ages, all stations in life, and all types of dispositions are forever forming associations," he wrote in *Democracy in America*. "There are not only commercial and industrial associations in which all take part, but others of a thousand different types—religious, moral, serious, . . . very general and very limited, immensely large and very minute."[4] Since Tocqueville's time, Americans' group memberships and the quality of community in the United States have drawn the attention of many scholars.[5] Lately, it is fair to say, students of community see it as troubled, beset by threats and challenges on many sides.

Here I want to consider one aspect of community life—the relationship between place and community—taking a close look at the places we treasure. In *Community on the American Frontier*, historian Robert V. Hine observes: "Wherever community thrived on the frontier it was framed by a sense of place."[6] A person who understood this in her bones was Laura Ingalls Wilder, who grew up on the edge of the Midwestern frontier during the 1870s and 1880s, accompanying her parents and three sisters as they migrated from place to place looking for better economic opportunities for their family. Four of Wilder's children's novels were set in De Smet, Dakota Territory, her "Little Town on the Prairie." Focusing as much as she did on the social groups and interactions that tied people together, she might just as easily have called it "the little community on the prairie."[7]

De Smet was a vigorous, active community of people that brought its residents together—young and old, better-off and poorer-off, town dwellers and farmers residing in the countryside—to address problems of common concern and to enjoy themselves in joint activities. The "little town on the prairie" was a highly social place. Wilder's novels describe Fourth of July celebrations, picnics, birthday parties, school exhibitions, church services, prayer meetings, ladies' aids, singing schools, spelling bees, political activities, "sociables," and "literaries" that brought out the entire town. However, not everything about the community was cast in a positive light in her books. Wilder reveals that town residents could be stupid, selfish, narrow-minded, and uncooperative. Some were not stellar contributors to the welfare of the community. But overall, the cooperativeness and sense of obligation that commonly prevailed in De Smet, according to Wilder, made it a desirable place to live, engendered optimism, and encouraged people to work together.[8]

Much of the community spirit depicted in Laura Ingalls Wilder's little town depended upon the places where it incubated—in stores on

Main Street, at the depot by the railroad tracks, in the church that her father helped build, and in the school she attended, which also served as a place for spelling bees, literary entertainments, school exhibitions, and a variety of other events. For a time, while her family was living on their homestead a mile or so southeast of town, Laura thought of the town as "a sore on the prairie," since it looked so forlorn and unfinished, in contrast with the majestic and colorful, wildflower-strewn countryside around it. Later, as she grew increasingly self-confident and became more involved in activities with children her own age, she changed her mind about it and came to like it. Much of the reason for her glowing memories of the town related to activities that she connected with particular places where social interaction occurred. She enjoyed attending church socials, spelling bees, local talent performances, singing school, and other such gatherings. Community for her was profoundly connected to place.[9]

Sinclair Lewis was another small town Midwesterner who probed the connection between place and community. His *Main Street*, published in 1920, conferred instant notoriety upon its author and set him on a path toward the Nobel Prize for literature. "Gopher Prairie," the fictional setting for his novel, was a reimagined version of Lewis's home town of Sauk Centre, Minnesota, whose population of about 3,000 was many times the size of Wilder's De Smet. Although his recollections of childhood mellowed over time, the picture of community that Lewis portrayed in his novel was almost unrelievedly bleak. His characters were, for the most part, dull, boring, narrow-minded, and mean-spirited.[10] On one thing, however, the two authors were in agreement: the quality of community in both towns depended heavily upon the buildings and places where community interaction took place.

Carol Kennicott's thirty-two minute stroll up and down Main Street at the beginning of the novel is perhaps the most famous walk ever taken by an American fictional character. Recently married to the town doctor and new to the community, she hoped to get a quick "fix" on the place and find out what she was going to be dealing with there. By the end of her walk, she was in despair: "Main Street with its two-story brick shops, its story-and-a-half wooden residences, its muddy expanse from concrete walk to walk, its huddle of Fords and lumber-wagons, was too small to absorb her." The adjectives Lewis employed to describe the places she observed reveals his condescending attitude about the town. The hotel was "shabby," its floors "unclean," and its chairs "rickety." The drug store had a "greasy" marble soda fountain and "pawed-over" piles of tooth-brushes, combs, and bars of soap. A grocery displayed "overripe" bananas and lettuce, the meat market "reeked" of blood, a jewelry shop offered "tinny-looking" wrist-watches, and the "fly-buzzing" saloon stank of "stale" beer. An alternative description of the town came from Bea Soren-son, a young woman just off a farm, who perceived the same places Carol Kennicott had just encountered in a much more positive light. But she was portrayed as naïve, and her sunnier view of the town was over-whelmed by the generally dour picture painted by Lewis throughout the rest of the book.[11]

Another Minnesotan, writing six decades after Sinclair Lewis pub-lished his classic novel, grew up not far from Sauk Centre and set his fic-tional town of "Lake Wobegon" just down the road from "Gopher Prairie." Based on my calculations, Garrison Keillor's imaginary town lies about thirty-two miles southeast of Lewis's, near St. Cloud, on the way to Min-neapolis. It is a far different kind of town, and many of the more positive images it presents are results of the places where community is cultivated in Lake Wobegon. For the past quarter-century on Keillor's Saturday afternoon radio program, "Prairie Home Companion," the lanky come-dian has been conjuring up images of his "home town," where "the women are strong, the men are good-looking, and the children are all above average." In his 1984 novel *Lake Wobegon Days*, he provided his most definitive description of the community. In that book he did not take his readers on any thirty-two minute walks, but he did begin it with a tour of the town, noting its major watering spots and gathering places— the grain elevator, Ralph's Grocery, Bunsen Motors, the Chatterbox Café, and two churches—Lake Wobegon Lutheran and Our Lady of Perpetual Responsibility, its Catholic counterpart.[12]

"It is a quiet town, where much of the day you could stand in the Middle of Main Street and not be in anyone's way," Keillor writes.[13] What some people refer to as "downtown" others call "up town." He gives names to the places—the "Ingqvist Block," "Union Block," "Security Block," "Farmers Block," and "Oleson Block"—which are "carved in sandstone or granite tablets set in the fancy brickwork at the top." In naming things or places, we usually attempt to confer dignity upon them and attest to their significance. In instances where we use terms belittling people or rendering them invisible, we harm and dehumanize them. In his books and radio programs dealing with Lake Wobegon, Keillor is both humorous and serious in his treatment of community, and sometimes his remarks are ironic or critical. But always he attests to its importance, the meanings it holds for people, and its ultimate significance. And to the degree that community actually exists in his world, it derives heavily from the places in which it takes form.

This insight has gained increasing recognition from a wide variety of social commentators in recent years. No one makes the point more persuasively than Ray Oldenburg did in his 1989 book *The Great Good Place*, which is subtitled "Cafes, coffee shops, community centers, beauty parlors, general stores, bars, hangouts and how they get you through the day."[14] He could have expanded the list to include church basements, parks, bowling alleys, baseball diamonds, high school gyms, skateboard ramps, malls, parking lots, senior centers, and many other places. Oldenburg understands the powerful need people have to associate with one another in places like "Cheers" on TV, where "everyone knows your name." These are locations where people can join together, cast aside concerns of work and household, and hang out simply for the pleasure of good company and lively conversation. They lie at the heart of community and reflect the vitality of its common bonds.

In contrast to settings of domesticity and work, Oldenburg calls attention to places of sociability, or "third places," which he thinks of as "the core settings of informal public life." They include a wide variety of public places where people can meet regularly, informally, voluntarily, and with great anticipation outside of the settings of home and work. "The wonder," Oldenburg writes, "is that so little attention has been paid to the benefits attaching to the third place. It is curious that its features and inner workings have remained virtually undescribed in this present age when they are so sorely needed and when any number of lesser substitutes are described in tiresome detail." Much has been written about encounter groups and sensitivity training, meditation and transcendentalism, jogging and exercise. But the simple remedy for loneliness, stress, and alienation that third places provide often gets overlooked, Oldenburg suggests, perhaps because they seem so commonplace.[15]

An excellent example of such a third place is the Main Street setting for the Saturday night ritual that was pervasive all over the Midwest and elsewhere in the United States from the 1920s through the 1950s. Farm folks would drive into town on Saturday nights to bring their cream and eggs, shop for groceries, and hang around to chat and schmooze with friends and neighbors. The practice of coming into town on market day antedated the internal combustion engine, but widespread improvements in roads and an explosion of automobile traffic during the 1920s converted Saturday night into the quintessential expression of community across a wide swath of the country. Today, if you ask someone who was born before Pearl Harbor if her town was a Saturday night town, the predictable reply will be, "Of course, it was! Everybody went to town on Saturday night!" Likely, she will also sigh wistfully and add that it would be nice if we could still find time for people of all ages and occupations to come together weekly to catch up on the news of the week, share juicy gossip, and discuss the latest developments in agriculture, fashion, the weather, and local sports teams.[16]

The huge importance of Saturday night went largely unnoticed at the time because it was so ordinary, such an integral part of people's lives. It was simply taken for granted. But with its disappearance, around the early 1960s, people started to realize how much they had lost. About that time, television, which had rapidly expanded its domination of people's evening hours during the previous decade, began to brush aside all of its competitors. The fifties had also witnessed the explosion of youth culture. It was no longer "cool" for teenagers to hang around with their parents, and now that more and more of them had access to their own cars, they no longer needed to tag along with the rest of the family for the drive into town on Saturday night.

Economic factors reinforced these changes in people's social habits. Milk producers and wholesale grocers moved in to control more and more of the processing and marketing of food, and local cream and egg buyers disappeared. These and other developments combined to kill off Saturday night, which is remembered by many today with nostalgia and wistfulness.

Back then, there were other activities, groups, and organizations that also contributed substantially to cooperative community, such as churches, schools, civic organizations, sports teams, and community fund drives. But Saturday night possessed the kinds of attributes that Ray Oldenburg's "great good places" have: regularity, informality, anticipation, and a commingling of many different kinds of people in a congenial setting. Going to town on Saturday night was relatively cheap, and it did not place pressures on people to perform. They needed merely to be themselves and enjoy hanging out with their friends and neighbors.

Saturday night, as long as it lasted, was very much connected to place. Activities on Main Street and beyond it were free-flowing and they spread out from block to block, taking place in shops, stores, grain elevators, pool halls, bowling alleys, people's cars, and on the sidewalks, in backroom card games, and over by the filling station. These were places to which people felt connected and from which they derived significant meaning. No wonder they remember Saturday night with such warm affection.

Unfortunately, the tenor of community life in recent decades has departed significantly from the kinds of close, personal ties and face-to-face interactions that characterized Saturday night—and community generally—in the past. Concern for the direction in which society is headed gets voiced in many quarters. Philip Slater characterizes ours as a "lonely society," Christopher Lasch calls it the "culture of narcissism," and Robert Hughes talks about a "culture of complaint."[17] Robert Bellah and his associates lament the decline of community spirit in America, Michael Sandel analyzes "Democracy's discontent," and Amitai Etzioni, the guru of community studies in this country, has sounded a call for its

12

renewal. Harvard political scientist Robert Putnam's influential 2000 book, *Bowling Alone: The Collapse and Revival of American Community*, further documents the decline of community participation during the last third of the twentieth century.[18]

If community indeed is in decline these days, it behooves us to pay attention to the problem and to search for solutions that will revive a sense of obligation and cooperation in people and nurture the kinds of conditions that may help revive its health and vitality. Many approaches are possible, and, as time goes by, creative solutions will present themselves. Here I wish to stress the importance of cultivating the kinds of places where community thrives.

People possess considerable control over the types of places where they live, work, play, enjoy leisure time, meet and interact with neighbors and fellow community residents, and fulfill their civic duties as responsible citizens. They can no longer afford to take their physical environments for granted. They need to pay careful attention to them and deliberately make choices that will enhance those environments and cultivate places where community can be practiced. In the process, people will confront limits and constraints, on one hand, and options and opportunities on the other. It is, of course, important to understand that, no matter what our situations are, there are certain givens that must be accepted and accommodated. On the other hand, multiple possibilities await those who possess imagination, flexibility, and the determination to take advantage of them. Some people resist rocking the boat because they are too intellectually lazy, too set in their opinions, or too lacking in imagination. Realism is required, but also idealism and openness to new possibilities. There are limits and constraints on what people can accomplish. The natural environment poses some of these, including the availability of natural resources, the kind of weather prevailing in a place, soil types, rainfall, and other environmental factors. Warm weather birds cannot live in North Dakota, and people averse to wet conditions should not settle in Seattle.

Historical circumstances also limit and shape the possibilities available in a particular community. Most towns in the Midwest are or once were railroad towns—a factor hugely important to their structure and development. Almost everywhere, the grid prevails in the arrangement of streets and physical layout. Most towns are laid out in similar fashion. Standard dimensions predominate for lots, streets, and alleys, resulting in familiar-looking buildings and blocks. Most stores in the business districts have 25-foot or 50-foot fronts, conforming to the dimensions of the lots on which they are situated. Most of them stand a story or two tall and are constructed of brick, wood, or stone. Most of them have a long, narrow feeling about them, extending back fifty to a hundred feet or more from the sidewalk. Within these standard dimensions, considerable variation exists, but clear limits normally restrict what an owner can do, at least with the original lot structures.[19]

Economic factors also play a crucial role in determining the possibilities available to a community. In a primarily agricultural economy, there are definite limits on what can be accomplished. Without other sources of income, the population of any given community is determined primarily by the number of farmers who depend upon it for services and products. Growth beyond that depends on developing industry and tourism and on redirecting community energy to other activities, such as schools, hospitals and clinics, nursing facilities, and entertainment venues. Transportation has always played a major role in town development. When the railroad was the most important connecting link to the outside world, the train depot was sometimes the most imposing or distinctive structure in town and often was a place where people gathered simply to engage in conversation or to watch people come and go. Grain elevators, lumberyards, livery stables, hotels, and other businesses located near the tracks were other distinctive gathering places. Economic factors thus provide both resources for and impose limits upon what a town is able do in constructing places that promote community.

Various characteristics of the population also influence what gets built and what gets used in a community. Norwegian and Swedish church buildings differ from those built by Germans and Poles.[20] As numbers of the elderly increase in a community, senior centers, nursing and assisted living facilities, and health care operations expand their operations.

Where sports are popular, high school football fields and basketball gyms are prominent and sports bars may come in. When people take pride in their communities and care about their appearances, backyards are tidy and sport a variety of decorative flowerbeds, wind chimes, and birdhouses, and people's houses and stores are attractive and invite people to gather and talk to one another.

So, there are many factors that influence and place limits on the level of interaction and quality of community that exist in a place. By the same token, communities possess many assets and resources that can be drawn upon to enhance their opportunities and expand their possibilities. These involve active choice on the part of the citizenry and require them to become involved and take ownership of their own home towns. People cannot afford to think only of themselves and their own families. They need to become aware of and responsible for the improvement of the quality of life of their entire community. In other words, they need to make the places where community happens pleasant, inviting, and conducive to conversation, interaction, and cooperative decision-making.

This is a matter of will and requires involvement and exertion. Attitude is everything. One can choose to be optimistic or pessimistic, hopeful or cynical, positive or negative, cooperative or divisive. People need to take it upon themselves to make situations work in their favor rather than against them. This is the good old American philosophy of pragmatism—probably the most distinctive contribution the United States has made to philosophy. It holds that we do not need to let conditions determine our fate; we can act boldly to alter our states of mind in ways that foster achievement and progress rather than stagnation and defeat.

Creativity is also highly relevant to the fate of community. People's ability to generate new ideas for enhancing economic development and the quality of life in a place will determine how they perceive their towns and how much they enjoy living in them. It requires imagination and creativity to establish a new business, make an elder program work, support a historical society, or induce a doctor to locate in town. Many things conspire to prevent people from thinking outside of well-worn patterns—safety, inertia, time constraints, pressures to conform, and inexperience. But people can choose to burst those bonds and be innovative.

Boldness, bravery, and willingness to try new things enhance the prospects of any community. Determination, willingness to sacrifice, and commitment to following through are necessary for success. Large amounts of time and effort are required to support volunteer fire departments, ambulance services, meals-on-wheels programs, and other cooperative efforts that enhance the lives of residents. These all require people to sacrifice some of their individual comfort for the good of the community. This is reciprocity in action. The motive behind such sacrifice and commitment is a generous one; people feel a sense of accomplishment through helping their neighbors and fellow human beings. But a sense of reciprocal obligation is also involved—by helping others, people express the wish or expectation that, in similar circumstances, others will come to their aid.

A fourth factor instrumental in promoting the quality of life in an community is the cooperative spirit, expressed in participation in such organizations as church youth groups, ladies aids, senior centers, Kiwanis clubs, business and professional women's clubs, political parties, and nature conservancy groups. Working alone, individuals can only accomplish so much. Cooperating in groups, they multiply their talents and potential for success. Examples abound. For instance, to help fund an expansion of their hospital, several years ago people in Clear Lake raised $400,000, a huge sum in a town of 1200 people. This was possible only by concerted effort and will. When large groups or an entire community work together as a unit, little can stop them.[21]

Finally, a community is enhanced by the places where its citizenry regularly meet and interact. These places usually emerge and develop naturally, with little thought given to how or why they exist. Families build homes in which to live, congregations build churches in which to worship, businesses build stores in which to serve their customers. And so it goes. In a capitalistic, freedom-loving society, the widest possible scope for individual choice is desirable. Within certain limits and government-imposed regulations, people can do largely as they please.

But individual satisfaction is not the only consideration when it comes to building community. "No man is an island," John Donne famously wrote. The counsel of wisdom is that in seeking one's own happiness and satisfaction, one will also look out for others and consider the welfare of the group. Individuals do not exist apart from society. A strong and healthy community contributes heavily to individual happiness and success. Place matters.

The places in which we live out our daily lives heavily influence how we think, feel, and ultimately prosper. Our attention needs to focus upon those kinds of places, and we need to consider what we can do to make them more attractive and inviting. Therefore, every town should make an inventory of the places where community happens. We don't have traditional Saturday nights anymore to bring people together informally in a ritual playing out of mutual interaction and reinforcement, so we need to try to recreate the functional equivalent of that community-creating occasion. People need to find or create more places that are inviting to people of all types—young and old, rich and poor, men and women, Democrats and Republicans, farmers and businessmen, Vikings fans and Bronco fans, and every other size, shape, and mentality. There they can come together to shoot the breeze, listen to each other, affirm each other, recognize each other's importance, and offer mutual aid and encouragement.

Such social interaction and mutual affirmation still occurs in the cafes, bars, bowling alleys, church basements, basketball gyms, quick stops, grain elevator offices, and grocery stores in many of our small towns. But these places are becoming increasingly rare. They are frequented less and less, as more and more of us remain at home, glued to the tube, or are too busy with our work, families, and other duties to sit down and schmooze with friends. Many factors feed into the decline of communal life, but one of them surely is that the kinds of "great good places" that Ray Oldenburg talks about in his book are in shorter and shorter supply.

We should make this our goal: to set aside more time to talk to our neighbors, inquire about their welfare, and offer our support when they need it. We need to make sure that there are places in town where community can be cultivated and that not all of our time is focused on our own individual goals. We need to make the enhancement of community a top priority, for in so doing we will not only advance the welfare of our fellow citizens, but we will do the best possible thing we can do to enhance our own lives.

Notes:

1. Yi-Fu Tuan, *Topophilia: A Study of Environmental Perception, Attitudes, and Values* (Englewood Cliffs, NJ: Prentice-Hall, 1974).

2. Louise Erdrich, "A Writer's Sense of Place," in *A Place of Sense: Essays in Search of the Midwest*, ed. Michael Martone (Iowa City: University of Iowa Press, 1988), 43.

3. Daniel J. Boorstin discusses the notion of consumption communities in *The Americans: The Democratic Experience* (New York: Vintage Books, 1974), 89-164. The Bender quotation is from *Community and Social Change in America* (Baltimore: Johns Hopkins University Press, 1982), 8.

4. Alexis de Tocqueville, *Democracy in America*, trans. George Lawrence, ed. J.P. Mayer (New York: Doubleday, Anchor Books, 1969), 523.

5. For a good historical summary of American thinking on the subject of community, see Bender, *Community and Social Change in America*.

6. Robert V. Hine, *Community on the American Frontier: Separate but Not Alone* (Norman: University of Oklahoma Press, 1980), 247.

7. Laura Ingalls Wilder, *Little Town on the Prairie* (New York: Harper & Row, 1941).

8. See John E. Miller, *Laura Ingalls Wilder's Little Town: Where History and Literature Meet* (Lawrence: University Press of Kansas, 1994).

9. John E. Miller, "Place and Community in Wilder's De Smet," ibid., 16-34.

10. Mark Schorer, *Sinclair Lewis: An American Life* (New York: McGraw-Hill, 1961), 286-97.

11. Sinclair Lewis, *Main Street* (1920, reprint New York: New American Library, 1961), 36-44 (quotation on p. 37).

12. Garrison Keillor, *Lake Wobegon Days* (New York: Viking, 1985), 1-3. The Sidetrack Tap, the site of a lot of the action in the community, gets introduced later in the book.

13. Ibid., 3.

14. Ray Oldenburg, *The Great Good Place: Cafes, Coffee Shops, Community Centers, Beauty Parlors, General Stores, Bars, Hangouts and How They Get You through the Day* (New York: Paragon House, 1989).

15. Ibid., 16, 20.

16. On the changing meaning of Saturday night for Americans, see Susan Orlean, *Saturday Night* (New York: Knopf, 1990).

17. Philip E. Slater, *The Pursuit of Loneliness: American Culture at the Breaking Point* (Boston: Beacon Press, 1970); Christopher Lasch, *The Culture of Narcissism: American Life in an Age of Diminishing Expectations* (New York: W.W. Norton, 1978); Robert Hughes, *Culture of Complaint: The Fraying of America* (New York: Oxford University Press, 1993).

18. Robert Bellah, et al., *The Good Society* (New York: Alfred A. Knopf, 1991); Michael J. Sandel, *Democracy's Discontent: America in Search of a Public Philosophy* (Cambridge, Mass.: Harvard University Press, 1996); Amitai Etzioni, *The Spirit of Community: The Reinvention of American Society* (New York: Simon & Schuster, 1993); Robert D. Putnam, *Bowling Alone: The Collapse and Revival of American Community* (New York: Simon & Schuster, 2000).

19. On the layout of towns, see John C. Hudson, *Plains Country Towns* (Minneapolis: University of Minnesota Press, 1985), 86-103; John W. Reps, *Cities of the American West: A History of Frontier Urban Planning* (Princeton: Princeton University Press, 1979), 390-454, 490-556.

20. Robert C. Ostergren, "The Immigrant Church as a Symbol of Community and Place in the Upper Midwest," *Great Plains Quarterly*, Vol. 1 (Fall, 1981), 225-38.

21. On recent efforts to promote community and civic participation, see Amitai Etzioni, ed., *New Communitarian Thinking: Persons, Virtues, Institutions, and Communities* (Charlottesville: University Press of Virginia, 1995); Theda Skocpol and Morris P. Fiorina, eds., *Civic Engagement in American Democracy* (Washington, DC: Brookings Institution Press, 1999); Robert Wuthnow, *Sharing the Journey: Support Groups and America's New Quest for Community* (New York: Free Press, 1994); Daniel Kemmis, *Community and the Politics of Place* (Norman: University of Oklahoma Press, 1990).

Discussion questions:

1. Do you agree with Alexis de Tocqueville, writing in the 1830s, that the tendency to form and participate in associations is a key feature of American life?

2. Draw a map of your town and identify the places where community occurs.

3. What are the "third places" in your town?

4. Has their number increased or decreased in recent years?

5. What kinds of third places do you think are lacking which would you would like to see established?

6. What kinds of people in your community, if any, get excluded from the third places that exist?

7. What can be done to improve the third places in your town?

Mourners

Ted Kooser

After the funeral, the mourners gather
under the rustling churchyard maples
and talk softly, like clusters of leaves.
White shirt cuffs and collars flash in the shade:
highlights on deep green water.
They came this afternoon to say goodbye,
but now they keep saying hello and hello,
peering into each other's faces,
slow to let go of each other's hands.

"Mourners," from Ted Kooser's *Delights & Shadows*, Copper Canyon Press, 2004, reprinted by permission of the author.

Discussion question:

1. What does this poem suggest to you about the pain and the promise of community?

The Land as a Model for Community: Biological, Ecological and Global Community

Nels H. Granholm

A species is successful if it reproduces itself and continues to adapt to an ever-changing environment. A species must achieve some kind of ecological balance with its surround, i.e., it must live in a manner which is sustainable not only for itself but for the other community members of its ecosystem. Herein lies one of our most fundamental human problems: we are not living in an ecologically sustainable manner. To sustain earth's resources, we need to come to accept that we humans are simply just one component of the global ecosystem. We are not somehow separate and therefore exempt from the rules of the ecosystem game. We are deeply embedded in nature but we mostly do not know it. If and when we truly acknowledge our partnership with nature and stop trying to have supremacy over it, we may then become bona fide members of the global ecosystem. We are an immature species. We must learn our fundamental ecological lessons before it is too late.

At present the human population, by virtue of its size and scope (over six billion of us), has a profoundly negative impact on nature. And we Homo sapiens represent but one small part, one of millions of species, of the great continuum of evolutionary life. As such, we share the ecological rules of engagement with our biotic brethren. The same rules that regulate the lives and ecosystems of nonhuman biota also constrain and regulate our lives. Like all other life, we must adhere to the rules of ecology to be successful as a species. Our current ecological problems stem in part from the fact that we, for one reason or another, divorce ourselves from the rules of ecology and ecological community. We will be mature and successful as a species only when we grasp the reality that we are part of and not separate from the global ecosystem.

Recently, I have become interested in global studies, i.e., phenomena related to the physical, biological, political, economic, cultural, and social aspects of how the world works. This is a very complex, interrelated, and vast subject area. One might ask how the discipline of global studies is in any way related to biology. This apparent leap to the global perspective is not as great as it would seem to be. It is a matter of simply extending ecological rules and principles to the global dimension. Like the old adage, "As General Motors goes, so goes the nation," we can say, "As the global ecology goes, so goes the health and well-being of the global biota —humans included." If we have a sustainable global ecology, we will have a healthy global biology and global community!

Virtually everything we possess comes initially from the physical earth. All goods and services we humans use come from natural resources. They are generally "extracted" in some sense from the greater environment. Think about that for a moment. This revelation is a true epiphany! Virtually everything we have, everything we wear, everything we use, everything we eat, and everything we can ever be is/was in some way extracted from the earth. Even the atoms that comprise the molecules of our bodies are derived from the earth. So, the socioeconomic world is a subset of the natural world, i.e., the economy is a subset of ecology. According to the *Online Etymology Dictionary* both words— economy and ecology—are derived from the Greek root "oikos" (meaning"home"or"hearth") or "oikonomia" (meaning "household manager"). Thus, it makes good sense to keep our economy and ecology in balance. One depends upon the other. We need our ecology to maintain our economy! It's that simple.

Because people are bona fide members of the natural world we, like all other biota, display habits of community, some good and some not so good. Due to our restless nature, inquisitiveness, creativity, and desire for better lives, we humans often make mini-Faustian bargains by our failure to recognize our impact on the environment. Each of us, by virtue of our lifestyle, causes ecological damage to the general environment. The amount of damage can be quantitatively assessed. The so-called "ecological footprint" is one such quantitative measure. We Americans have an ecological footprint about 20 times greater than that of a native person living in New Guinea or the Amazon Basin. To put it another way, if all the people on earth lived as we do in the West, we would need the resources of about four to five additional earths to provide the necessary resources. Sooner or later, as is the case in all Faustian bargains, those who have gone astray must return to a more balanced, stable, and healthy community as defined by ecological models in the natural world. Will we do this voluntarily? We will if we understand the principles of community and ecology!

One of the most profound expressions of community in the biological world is the fact that all life is descended from an original life form that has evolved over three billion years. Because of our shared evolutionary past, we humans and all global biota are truly related. As John Steinbeck once said, "All things are one thing, and one thing is all things."[1] With respect to the genetic information that all biota share, this is truly the case with the world's biota. The genes of all biota are incredibly similar. Thus, we are a community based on our shared inheritance as verified by the genetic similarities between all biota. We are truly kin to all of the biological community!

By virtue of the similarity of our DNA—the base sequences or nucleotides that comprise our genes—all biotic species, from trees to green algae to blue whales, hummingbirds, and lovely orchids are biotic members of one continuous community of life. That continuity and community is observed within the physical essence of all life—the DNA! I can think of no better physical evidence to support the notion that all biota comprise one huge evolutionary family. Other data to support the contention that all biota are related come from the analysis of developmental or embryological patterns. As we survey the patterns of animal embryology, we observe the same recurring developmental themes.

Human embryos have gill slits and tails. Why? Because the basic developmental plan of all vertebrates over the last few hundred million years or so has been honed to perfection via natural selection.

When something works successfully in nature, it is preserved. We find little if any excess or extraneous baggage in nature. Thus amphibians, reptiles, birds, fish, and mammals all undergo the same basic early developmental pathways and diverge only later in development to specify—to become various species of vertebrates like fish and reptiles. With regard to the early embryology of all vertebrates, patterns of embryology appear to replicate an overall evolutionary plan. Vertebrate organisms undergo developmental stages similar if not identical to those vertebrate organisms from which they evolved, i.e., there is a significant conservation of developmental mechanisms. Finally, as adults, all biota share features in common—genetic code, behaviors, mobility, modes of conducting basic metabolism, strategies for getting along in life, reproductive similarities and many others. We are all related.

In the 19th Century, two German scientists, Schleiden and Schwann, advanced the cell theory, that all life is related by virtue of the fact that we are all composed of cells. Although cells have vastly different functions, they are all members of the same cellular community. All cells in any organism exist in balance and in equilibrium with other cells. They are all members of one large, integrated, and coordinate community. Each cell exists for the benefit of the community at large. However, when cells are damaged, they sometimes do not act as members of the larger community, but become rogue individual cells. These conditions lead to pathologic or disease states. Unless a balance (homeostasis) can be achieved by community compensatory mechanisms commonly known as homeostasis, death ensues.

The social, colonial insects such as bees and termites have often been compared to organisms, with each individual likened to a single cell. Curiously, when working together to support the larger super-organism, these colonial insects represent superb models of community—all the members of the community work together for the good of the whole. Analyses of behavioral patterns suggest that colonial insects are "hard wired" to conduct highly specific functions. For example, some are worker bees, others attend to the needs of the queen, and still others carry on as soldier bees or drones. Although each individual bee of the hive is an autonomous organism, it rarely exercises its autonomy. For the most part, each individual behaves as a true member of the community— carrying out its particular social function as a good and truly dependable soldier, never rebelling, never plotting a mutiny, never complaining, and never questioning its role. Because each individual is driven to act for the good of the group, together they provide a truly compelling model for community!

Just as all life is part of one vast DNA community, we are all community by virtue of our evolution from common ancient biological life or primordial organisms. There are two strong bodies of data to support the idea that all life has evolved from one primordial organism—DNA sequence data and embryological data. The latter demonstrate this truth by carefully tracing the developmental states of organisms from fertilized eggs to fully formed and definitive embryos—mouse, frog, turtle, bird, or human.

One of Darwin's unique, singular, and profound contributions was his formulation of the theory of evolution based on natural selection. During his five-year circumnavigation of the world (1831-1836) in the HMS Beagle, Darwin discovered the mechanism of natural selection as the ultimate driving force for evolution. Natural selection is perhaps the most singular and fundamental concept of all biology, because it explains and predicts virtually all biological phenomena. Just as species evolve based on nature's selection of the most biologically adapted or "fit" members of their population, ecosystems may evolve in similar ways. Thus, any analysis of community and biology will benefit from knowledge of how natural selection acts on community and ecosystems.

Ecosystems consist of two components 1) a cast of biotic characters (plants and animals) that comprise the living community and 2) physical or abiotic features (climate, soils, location, elevation, slope, direction from the sun, hydrology, neighboring features, temperature, etc.) that comprise the nonliving community in which those cast members must live and survive. Ecosystems are self-regulating. They tend to fluctuate and eventually restore themselves to some level of healthy ecological balance. If left alone, i.e., not severely traumatized by human or other destructive activity, they can care for themselves. And they evolve.

Because ecosystems possess mechanisms which allow them to compensate for stress, they can and often do recover from stress. However, if the stress is ongoing and chronic, an ecosystem, just like an organism, will have a classic stress response. It will sense the stress in Stage One. In Stage Two, the ecosystem will attempt to compensate for the stress. If the stress is acute and not prolonged, compensatory mechanisms will allow the ecosystem to successfully adjust, and damage may not be permanent. However, if there is a prolonged stress, compensatory mechanisms may become exhausted (Stage Three). Severe alterations of the ecosystem, and even demise or death (Stage Four) may ensue. Generally speaking, loss of ecosystems results in the demise of many members of the biotic community.

There are various types of ecosystems—from the head of a pin, to deep ocean trenches, to Antarctic ecosystems, to something like a prairie ecosystem. Common denominators of all ecosystems include nonliving (abiotic) and living (biotic) components. Abiotic aspects include physical factors (temperature, elevation, rainfall, climate, sun conditions, longitude/latitude, soils, and many others). Biotic components include the totality of all plants and animals and all other types of life within the community. The sun that ripples through and sustains life, and drives all ecosystems, energizes both the abiotic surround and the biotic community. Few recognize and appreciate the process of photosynthesis, the conversion of sun's energy into glucose, as fundamental to all life! The fundamental principles of ecosystem operation remain the same, i.e., energy flows from the sun to all the members of the community—to the plants and then in the form of food to the invertebrata, and ultimately to the larger animals (vertebrata) at the tops of the food chains. The land, a subset of all terrestrial ecosystems, retains or loses ecological health, depending upon our biological use and our philosophical views of the land as fundamentally instrumental or intrinsic in nature.

Logically, then, the more we know about ecosystem dynamics and what it means to achieve ecosystem health, the more we tend to view land not only as an instrument for our use but also as an entity possessing immense value in and of itself. As a mature species, at home with our place in the world, we ought to view land and ecosystems as having deep and fundamental intrinsic value—the so-called "deep ecology" view.

The term "land" connotes many things to many people. Most importantly, land is the fundamental natural resource of the collective ecosystems we all enjoy. As the numbers and variety of biotic community members increases within ecosystems, so does their overall resiliency and health. A robust three-dimensional web with numerous healthy connections and many ramifying, interlinking, and reinforcing strands is a healthy ecosystem. Given a sufficiently robust three-dimensional web, the loss of a few strands does not result in the collapse of the web. A healthy ecosystem enjoys a rigorous three-dimensional web of interactions linking all the individual community members. The greater the extent of the three-dimensional web, the more balanced, tough, resistant to change, and permanent the ecosystem will be. Environmental insults of various kinds cause ruptures in the strands of the web. Given a healthy and robust network of community members with an elaborate three-dimensional web, an ecosystem can withstand considerable trauma. However, there are limits.

As humans with the cognitive power to understand the complexity of ecosystems, what keeps them healthy and what makes them endangered, we are in a position to treat our ecosystems with respect and dignity. We should want to do this for two reasons. One, it is the morally right thing to do, because all nonhuman biota have a right to live out their lives according to their genetic and evolutionary destinies, just as humans do. And two, it is the practical thing to do, because healthy ecosystems are essential for our very survival.

There are two principal ways we view any natural resource such as land—instrumentally and intrinsically. By far our most common and comfortable approach is to view the land as having instrumental value. In this way of thinking, land is simply an instrument for deriving benefits such as food, shelter, energy, clothing, minerals, recreation, and hunting. In the instrumental view, a natural resource is like a carpenter's hammer. A hammer, although beautifully designed to fulfill a given purpose, is merely an instrument used to pound nails or pry boards apart. If something happens to that hammer, if it gets lost of destroyed, then it is a bit of an inconvenience and perhaps an additional expense. But nothing of any real fundamental value has been lost. Hammers can be replaced. There is nothing particularly special about a hammer. It is just an instrument we use to do a job, as is a natural resource when viewed instrumentally. But there's another way to view that resource, the intrinsic view of land.

In this way of thinking, land is different than a hammer. It has value embedded within it. It is like a twenty-dollar gold piece; twenty dollars worth of gold are embedded within the coin. Similarly, land has value in and of itself. It has inherent worth regardless of how we humans might view it. In short, land has some kind of right independent of what we humans deem its use should be. Many would argue that this is a weak claim and therefore not a very compelling argument. Where can we go to derive support for this argument of land having intrinsic worth? To what authorities can we appeal?

Let us consider a superb ecologist and recognized conservationist, Dr. Aldo Leopold, who took a balanced view, both instrumental and intrinsic, toward the natural world. In the mid-20th Century, Leopold urged us to stop thinking about land use as solely a question of economic expediency (the instrumental view) and think of it as a matter of what is ethically right, proper, and respectful for the good of the ecosystem (the intrinsic view). Leopold urged us to live our lives showing respect for nature but to make use of nature in careful, cautious, and minimally disruptive ways (an enlightened instrumentality). At the same time Leopold encouraged us to consider nature as having value beyond our knowing and to show restraint and respect for nature's claims to live out individual biotic destinies (an enlightened intrinsic view). Leopold's fundamental or "golden rule" sums up his overall position: "A thing is right when it tends to preserve the integrity, stability, and beauty of the biotic community. It is wrong when it tends otherwise."[2] This profound statement captures the essence of both the instrumental and the intrinsic positions. It also allows us to define ethically right action both scientifically (we can measure integrity and stability) and spiritually (we can grapple with explanations of beauty). Finally, it makes humans responsible to ecosystems. In addition to being instrumentally valuable to humans, ecosystems ought to be preserved because they possess an intrinsic claim and a valid ethical claim to be allowed to fulfill their collective genetic and evolutionary destinies.

In summary, it is important to explore various concepts and hierarchies of "biological community" to determine common denominators of healthy communities. Analyses of various levels of biological community from DNA sequence data, cell theory, embryological patterns, behavior of colonial insects, and ecosystem dynamics lead to three major conclusions. One, all life on this earth is highly related. Whether we like it or not, we are all related. So, we ought to behave like good relatives. Two, life flourishes when it is able to carry out its genetic and evolutionary destiny. Healthy biological communities such as ecosystems retain their health and well-being when allowed to function according to their optimal physical and biological rules and constraints, not according to those superimposed upon them by humans overzealous in their desire to make instrumental use of ecosystem resources. And three, as humans we ought to pledge to exercise appropriate judgment with respect to the delicate balancing act of viewing nature instrumentally and intrinsically. In this respect, we ought to follow the "integrity, stability, and beauty" dictum of Aldo Leopold.

Leopold once said, "Breakfast comes before ethics."[3] In that vein, let us recognize that it is entirely appropriate to use land instrumentally for our livelihood and survival. But let us also recognize the delicate balance between using the resource and preserving the resource. We intuitively know that in the long run, our only sustainable approach is to treat the land with respect by somehow developing an intrinsic valuation to complement our instrumental approach. There are two fundamentally sound reasons for adopting this approach. The first is that it is the morally right thing to do. The second is that it is the most practical or pragmatic thing to do. In the words of Joseph Wood Krutch, ". . . To live healthily and successfully on the land we must also live with it. We must be part not only of the human community but of the whole community . . . it is not a sentimental but a grimly literal fact that unless we share this terrestrial globe with creatures other than ourselves, we shall not be able to live on it for long . . . You may if you like think of this as a moral law . . . if we do not permit the earth to produce beauty and joy, it will in the end not produce food either."[4]

Notes:

1. Personal communication from David Allan Evans.

2. Leopold, Aldo. *A Sand County Almanac and Sketches Here and There*. New York. Oxford University Press. 1949.

3. Tanner, Thomas. *Aldo Leopold: The Man and His Legacy*. Ankeny, Iowa. Soil Conservation Society of America. 1987.

4. Krutch, Joseph W. *The Great Chain of Life*. Boston. Houghton Mifflin. 1956.

Discussion Questions:

1. In *Small is Beautiful*, Ernest Schumacher suggests that there is something fundamentally healthy and essential about small "economies of scale." Do you agree? Why or why not?

2. How might one's relationship to the land, one's rootedness, drive or sustain one's desire to live in small communities rather than in cities?

3. What are the disadvantages of living in rural areas? Are these significant or trivial disadvantages?

Rosebud Reservation

Lydia Whirlwind Soldier

island of refuge, homeland
sunshine in an alien world
sweet tender rosebuds
and painted sunsets
bald eagles prayers
in the golden light of morning
voices gathered in strong heart songs
in the midst of it all, I am

defying and rooted strong
on ancient stone
healing power of this land
humble heart and bowed head
I stand
reflection of grandma's dream
hold close my refuge
my reservation
my homeland

Discussion Questions:

1. What are some common assumptions about Indian reservations? Compare and contrast those assumptions with what this poem expresses.

2. How does this poem define "community"? Is this consistent with your definition of it? Why or why not?

Dwelling on the Land

Dennis Bielfeldt

I

Demographics declare that rural communities are dying. There are fewer people living on working farms, fewer towns supported by such farms, and fewer people making their primary income in agriculture. Those remaining on farms and in small towns often have limited cultural and economic opportunities. While many see the decline of rural life as a necessary consequence of technological and social progress, and ultimately no great loss to society, others believe that something important will vanish if the decline continues. But what is that something? Is it the correct use of land? Is it human dignity and value? Is it economic self-sufficiency? Is it community itself?

There are many ways to document what perishes in the decline of rural communities. Unfortunately, while environmental, sociological, economic, geographic and even political analyses can aid in understanding what has been lost, none of these analyses go deep enough, for none really call us to a re-collection of that rich fabric of meanings comprising what it was to dwell upon the land. To bring to light the world of land dwelling, another type of inquiry is required, an inquiry that attempts to articulate and open that world for others to see and understand.[1] In this brief essay, I shall try to be attentive to Being as it once revealed itself in the world of rural beings, in the doings of those who dwelt and built upon the prairie.[2] My thesis is that in leaving the land, human beings lose a fundamental way of dwelling in the world; they lose their ancient, deep moorings to earth, sky, God and self.

A philosophical exploration of rural living is especially difficult today because the world we wish to examine is no longer fully present. It survives in memories and in conversation and in those places that still faintly sway to the pulse of Being that was once carried on the prairie winds.[3] But we must not let the loss of direct access to that world dissuade us from the exploration. Our collective memory still provides us glimpses of authentic rural life, of a life that continues faintly to beckon us, but which now is for us forever closed.

II

As a child, I had a clearer perception than I now do of the cycle of days and seasons. Different days had different orders and characters. The emptiness of Sunday afternoon differed from the bustle of Monday morning. The darkness of winter nights contrasted starkly with the long July evenings when the sun glowed weakly in the northwest as I searched for sleep. The same is true of space. Hills were larger in those days, snow was deeper, and alfalfa more fragrant. Children do often see more clearly than adults. Perhaps this is because children don't yet know how to put to use the things in their world; they have not yet learned about an object's social, economic or political properties. Prior to learning to use and categorize, children have the grace to encounter things in their *originality*, to understand them immediately within their fabric of fundamental meanings. For most of us, childhood offers the best chance to encounter things on their own, to meet things yet untrammeled, things liberated in their originality to be what they truly are. To comprehend what it was to dwell in rural community, we need the eyes of the child; we need to peer back beyond the "what-is-it-for-ness" and "how-does-it-come-to-be-ness" to rediscover the "what-it-is-ness."

Growing up on an Iowa farm, I was blessed to come to an understanding of self within a web of meanings in the space between the earth and the sky, a space shared with mortal beings like me limited by an eternal realm unlike me. To live on the prairie is to have privileged access to the ground of our world, for fundamentally our world does emerge in the space between earth and sky, mortals and the divine.[4]

As a child I learned about the earth. Though I knew nothing about soil types and productivity, cost per acre, and amortization and depreciation schedules, I learned what it is to be earth. Weeding the garden, walking soybeans, baling hay, picking sweet corn, and burying dead lambs disclosed what is to be earth, to be that from which things arise and return, to be that upon which things take shape and present themselves. Any attempt to understand world apart from earth necessarily distorts the nature of world. Our worlds, the webs of fundamental meaning in which we find ourselves, are grounded in earth, and thus earth is implied even in urban worlds. Even those living in cities have a faint apprehension of the "edges" of their world, a recollection of that from which buildings emerge. On the farm, I quickly learned the primacy of the earth, and the way in which earth links to the diverse things in one's everyday world.

On the farm one also knows deeply the expanse of the sky. Farm life is connected profoundly to the cycles of seasons and weather. Rain falls to water the earth. Daily the sun makes a trek from east to west, pausing in the center of the sky to heat the ground from which the plants emerge. The snows fall, covering roads, and are driven by winter winds into banks that make entry into barns difficult. On dry spring days, the sky commands the strong southerly winds that dislodge the earth from its proper place, sending its black soil into the sky and darkening the sun. Even people in the city have a dim apprehension of sky as the place to which the buildings yearn. Sky calls plants and buildings from the earth to itself. Especially tall buildings are said even to "scrape" that sky by which they are called.

For the farmer, weather is not merely some meteorological fact, but that which affects the health of crops, the maturation of the corn as it seeks the sky. Rain is the lifeblood of what emerges from the earth. The meaning of rain is found in its ability to raise crops, to bring water to self, to *threaten* and *comfort*. Storms arise. Their meaning is apparent: they bring life, yet threaten with hail and wind. Storms gather in the west and march towards us; they confront us as the possibility of there no longer being crops seeking the sky. From the sky comes that which threatens the very possibility of crops giving homage to sky. Men and women dwelling upon the prairie are forever related to that which gives sustenance and can destroy. Like the god Shiva, the sky both nurtures and destroys.

But rural people do not lead solitary existences within a static fabric of meanings between earth and heaven; they move also within worlds that include others who themselves have worlds. They dwell with others who, like themselves, dwell between the earth and sky in vague anticipation of the impermanence of their dwelling. To be a human being is to be aware of one's mortality. *To be* is to be *timed*. All of us are timed beings, for our being is sketched out upon the canvas of nothingness. Only in knowing that we are not forever do we confront who it is we are. Only within the context of our own end do we grasp the text of our present existence. The realization of our death generates our meaning within time. Dwelling between earth and sky, we encounter the earth as that reservoir of being from which we come and toward which we move. The earth constantly reminds us of our timed existence, the brevity in which we dwell. We dwell with others in a timed solidarity. In this solidarity, we expose our own world to the dwelling of others, finding our world affected by their dwelling, locating our world in the context of theirs. On the farm, one encounters the commonality of worlds that becomes community. Mortals occupy a common place. In encountering the duality of earth and sky, men and women experience a prairie communion of commonality.[5]

Finally, living with others between earth and sky beckons transcendence. To know earth as origin and terminus, to know sky as source, to know self and others as not-having-to-be, is to be transported toward transcendence. On the farm one knows profoundly the basic fact of biological existence: we transitory things must die. But unlike the cattle, hogs, and sheep, our being consists in an awareness of the possibility of us having no more awareness. The corpses of farm animals remind us of the corpses we shall someday be. Yet we mortals persistently project ahead of ourselves possibilities of being. To think beyond the corpse is to enter the province of divinity. What remains when all passes? Mortals relentlessly think out beyond the possibility of there being no more possibilities. For us, such thinking is encountered as limit. It is a thinking that says, "Halt, You cannot progress beyond here." Divinity is the phenomenon of the "not" which judges all thinking beyond the possibility of there being no more possibilities. It is the continuing confrontation with the pushing beyond. It is the surpassing.

III

Looking out across the cornfield that one has planted and tended, one is already inside a world of meanings. The field of corn is not merely gross income input, but is what it primitively is. The corn rises to the sky, to the place from which the rains fall. In seeking the sky, the corn exhibits the polarity between the earth from which it emerges and the sky that summons its fruition. Walking down the cornrows, one is "close" to the plants, for they grow and develop just as man and woman do. Born of the earth, both seek the sky that draws them forth. Moreover, just as man and woman tend the corn, so too do they care for Be-ing, for that which calls forth their own lives. Human beings tend that from which they have come.

In the sheep barn in the middle of the night, one watches as fluid-covered lambs emerge from the waters of their births. Ewes, themselves born of earthly waters, act now as the gates through which new life springs forth, life ready to extend upright and take first faltering steps under the sky. Human beings dwell close to ewes and lambs, understanding that they too emerge from earthly waters, that they too were dried by the dawning sun, and that in this process were freed to take their first steps. As we mortals tend to the births of animals, we listen attentively to the faint sounds of that which births our own attendings. Where and what is that primordial Be-ing from which our attentive be-ing arose? Who first cared for those who care?

Watching the bloated heifer laboring for her last breaths presages our own final battle. Helplessly, we attend she who only two days ago was fattening contently in the feedlot. Her death means disposal of the corpse. In a bygone time prior to EPA regulations, we could bury such hapless beasts on our own land.[6] While the sky looked on, we dug the hole with the tractor loader and deposited the lifeless body into an earth that gladly received her.

We are close to the animal, for in tending to her we again encounter our own plight. Our lives move from the womb to the tomb, from earth to earth under the gaze of the heavens that called us once to be. We stare out beyond the sky, awaiting messages from those whom we are not. Why is there something and not just nothing? What is it to be me, the one who stands upon earth, under sky, marking apprehensively the passing of the days?

IV

What was communal life like in past rural communities? Recall a typical Saturday night in a small town. Mother would get the children ready and she and Father would load them into the car to make the short trip into town. Because all the stores were open, they would need to come early if they wanted to park on Main Street. Getting out of the car, they would begin a slow walk on the sidewalk. Everyone knew Father. In the course of walking one hundred feet, he may have talked to the cornsheller man, the seedcorn dealer, the sprayer person, and three neighbors. Mother and children would soon tire of the slow pace and head toward the department store. In the days before Wal-Marts and K-marts, towns actually had such stores. Standing at a cash register as ancient as she herself was stood Lizzie, the clerk at the store and the oldest person the children had ever seen. Greetings were exchanged; Lizzie knew everyone and everyone knew Lizzie. Talking to people was important in the small town. Women's talk was of baking and cleaning; men conversed about crops, sows, and machinery. The dealings in which one found one's daily bearings were recalled and discussed on these evenings.

While Mother met women at the department store, Father stopped at the tavern for an obligatory beer or two. In the pool hall men congregated and spoke out their farm frustrations and joys. They reviewed, rehearsed, and rethought that which had confronted them during the day. In the to-and-fro movement of conversation that recollected past situations in which they found themselves, farmers saw different possibilities for doing the tasks lying before them. Electric fence could be strung this way because it didn't work right the last time. One might try planting soybeans this year without another disking because last year it got so wet that it was difficult to break up the dried clods. Perhaps one could get by laying corn aside the third time instead of doing a fourth cultivation. In the dialectic of conversation, men came to an understanding of their being upon the farm. Oftentimes, inventiveness and even daring took place in those conversations. Why not drive the tractor at night and fish while they bite? Dwelling upon the land between earth and sky demanded communicative existence. In speaking with each other, men and women found their orientation among earth, sky, other mortals and gods.

It is precisely because we no longer remember the primordial facts of existence that we no longer can speak out that existence. Conversely, because we no longer speak out our existence, we can no longer recall its primordial facts. Television and other media distract us into the numbing security of everyday superficiality. The flicker of TV screens reveals our penchant for distraction. We no longer want to know our primordial place or grasp our connections with earth, sky, humans, and gods. We seek to anesthetize ourselves from our mortal plight. Instead of dealing with existence by conversing and dwelling, we ignore it and concentrate upon the task of engineering for ourselves better lives.

Real communication arises from commonality and drives to communion. Even though conversation on Saturday nights did not often seek overtly to explore the subjectivity of the other, such conversation nonetheless affirmed the other by bespeaking the common world in which both speaker and hearer dwelt. All understood the threads of possibilities woven into the common fabric of life between earth and sky. While an urban community built upon true conversation is perhaps possible, most often life in the cities is a matter of superficial association and mere talk. Instead of dwelling in a common fabric between earth and sky, human beings associate in practiced alienation from the earth from which they emerged and to which they shall return, the sky which called them forth, other mortals with whom they share a common destiny, and the gods who eternally confront them. But land dwellers know full well the meaning of earth and sky, and thus they understand life as contingent and the divine as necessary. We pass away, the sky remains. Mortals are to earth as the sky is to God.

V

Perhaps what vanishes in the perishing of rural life is the attitude of what the Germans call *Gelassenheit*, that is, the posture of the "letting go" of things. Christians once knew that to follow Christ in freedom they needed to let go of worldly attachments. One understood freedom in Christ only when one "let go" of attachments outside Christ. Similarly, to understand what an object really *is*—to "free" it to be what it is—one must "let go" of one's attachment to it. To let go of a thing is to free it to be what it is; to let it go is to gain the thing back *as* the thing it is. To let go of a thing is no longer to seek to engineer its place within one's world, but rather to allow the thing to be what it primordially *is*. Consequently, letting go allows us to dwell within a world already given, within that pre-engineered world that is already our deepest and closest world. Really to know what it is to live on the farm demands that one cease calculating, for a time, how things might be used economically. One really only discovers what alfalfa is when one lets go of its economic value. Corn and cattle reveal themselves precisely in their disconnection from agribusiness. To grasp the being of that closeby involves letting it be what it is. One ignores the otherness of a thing in the calculation of how it can be of human value.

Just as one can never escape natural language in the construction of artificial languages, so one can never escape the natural world in the engineering of other worlds. The natural world is precisely the relationship of all objects liberated to be the objects they are. Such a world is always already there *for* the one who finds her bearings within it. There is no activity of finding one's way that is not at the same time a finding of one's way within things sometimes hidden, but capable of liberation through profound attentiveness. Only those with the eyes to see can see.

Dwelling between earth and sky as one who will not always be frees things to be what they are. Out in the cornfield in autumn watching flocks of ducks and geese overhead, one realizes perhaps how little of life can finally be plotted and controlled. Maybe our farm ancestors had access to being in ways that we can scarcely recollect. What would it be like to live life knowing that one would die upon the land upon which one dwelt, that no amount of work could bring about a qualitatively different kind of life off the land, that hard work and ingenuity would not result in acquisition of great wealth and its concomitant change of lifestyle? When illusions of the future are destroyed, one is freed to contemplate present realities: plants, animals, soil, weather, finitude, and God.

In the vanishing of rural life, we see accelerated the loss of human moorings to earth and sky. In the perishing of such a life we increasingly forget our own being, a being that primordially is in its awareness of death, a being that projects even beyond death to that which ultimately is death to death, to that which endures in the face of countless deaths. The excitement and distraction of life in the city often clouds our apprehension of what it is to be; it obscures and often suppresses entirely the fundamental question: Who *am* I?

As the depopulation of rural America continues and the prairie winds reclaim that which was once their own, human beings progressively forget that Be-ing which first gave humans their own being. Hunkered down in carefully-crafted trenches, we humans believe we escape the icy gale which blows in from our own futures. But it is illusion. Would that we could recognize such illusions and be claimed again by the prairie winds.

Notes:

1. I am using the term "world" to refer to the sum total of meanings in which one dwells. Consequently, world is the immediacy of meaning encountered and employed in one's everyday routines and activities. This notion of world, inherited from the idea of a "life world" (*Lebenswelt*) in Husserl, was developed by Martin Heidegger.

2. "To be attentive to" is "to deeply listen or scrutinize." One scrutinizes Be-ing; one is attentive to "to-beness" itself as it is revealed in the activities of rural dwellers.

3. Readers familiar with Heidegger will recognize some central assumptions of this essay. First, I presuppose the legitimacy of the connection between phenomenology and ontology. Phenomenology is concerned with that which discloses itself in its immediacy for consciousness, while ontology deals with the study of being. I assume that what shows itself pre-reflectively to consciousness, shows itself as what it is in itself. See Martin Heidegger, *Being and Time* (New York: Harper, 1962) 58-63. Also, I opt for the attitude adopted by the later Heidegger in encountering Being. Instead of trying to grasp the contour of Being by analyzing Dasein (the being, who in its being, has

being at issue), the mature Heidegger is content merely to document Being as it is encountered in world and language. For an early, but classic treatment of Heidegger's turn from phenomenological grasping to thoughtful response see William Richardson, *Heidegger: Through Phenomenology to Thought* (The Hague: Martinus Nijhoff, 1962). Third, I think Heidegger's notion of the Fourfold is immensely suggestive. Heidegger discusses the Fourfold of earth, sky, mortals and gods in his essays "The Thing," and "Building Dwelling Thinking." See Martin Heidegger, *Poetry, Language, Thought*, 1st Harper Colophon ed. (New York: Harper & Row, 1975). Finally, I suppose that Heidegger's analysis of Dasein as *Sein zum Tode* (Being-unto-death) is correct. We are our possibilities of being. The possibility of having no more possibilities is a deeply significant possibility for human beings.

4. The sense of "emerge" must be understood phenomenologically. The fabric of meanings encountered immediately in everyday existence arises within the more fundamental cluster of meanings of the down here, the up above, the encounter with others like me and with that transcending me entirely. All of our meaningful activity discloses itself against this more primitive orientation of meaning.

5. One might ask where other creatures are found in this fourfold of earth, sky, mortals and gods. Are farm animals more the stuff of mortals or are they of the earth? While different people locate them in different spheres, in my youth, rural people routinely understood the encounter with animals as an encounter with something of the earth. That this attitude is changing exemplifies the historicity of human existence and the phenomenological project itself.

6. The disposal of animals on one's own land has been prohibited for many years on our Iowa family farm.

Discussion Questions:

1. To what extent is Wordsworth's famous "the child is father of the man" statement applicable to this essay?

2. "As my eyes search the prairie, I feel the summer in the spring." What might the author of this essay have in common with the anonymous Anishinabe singer of that song? Do you relate to how they seem to feel?

3. Is what you think of as "nature" necessary for your human development? If not, why not? If so, why?

4. In "Fern Hill," the poet Dylan Thomas speaks longingly of that portion of his childhood which was "once below a time," before he was clock-conscious. What attitudes toward time do you find in this essay? Do you agree or disagree with those attitudes?

5. What, if anything, do memories of origins contribute to community and community development?

6. According to the author of this essay, what kinds of processes are important for individuals? For communities?

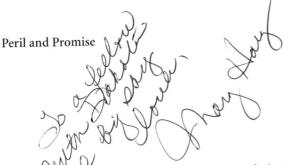

"Houses are like sentinels in the plain."
N. Scott Momaday

Up on the Roof:
A Rural Way of Being

Mary A. Haug

On the roof,
the only place I know,
where you just have to wish
to make it so.
Up On The Roof (Goffin/King)

"Place is space infused with meaning," wrote Lois Phillips Hudson, an author and scholar who came of age in Depression-era North Dakota.

The space infused with meaning in my life is the prairie and rolling hills of Lyman County, South Dakota, some 20 miles southwest of the Missouri River. I learned to know and love this landscape from the double-pitched rooftop of a rectangular, red wooden granary in the center of our farmyard. To my father, the granary represented the riches of land, given some years freely and plentifully, and in other years wrenched from parched and reluctant soil. In good years, my father would slide the wide doors of the granary open, back the truck into the alley between the grain bins that lined both walls, and fill the bins with truckloads of wheat until they overflowed and grain fell to the floor, making small piles of dinner for the mice that lived in the corners and the brown sparrows that roosted in the rafters. In my childhood, the granary offered me the gifts of sanctuary and solitude and I spent long summer days perched on its slanted shingled roof, daydreaming and imagining.

I lost my place on the granary roof the summer my father died. Having no experience in life-altering sorrow, I believed those who assured me that the ritual of the rosary and the funeral, as well as the support of family and friends would guide me through the grief process and bring an end to the sadness. And yet, something was wrong. For many years following the long, agonizing August of my father's dying, I had a recurring dream in which I searched for him driving the back road to our farm, certain he stood in the fields waiting for me. The dream never varied. As I recall it now, I am driving north out of Reliance on Highway 47 toward Medicine Butte, a site of healing power and wisdom for the Lakota, and for me, a reassuring landmark by which I always measured the distance from home.

I turn east at the cemetery, moving past the graves of my ancestors buried on the Catholic side, separated from the Protestant side by an invisible, inviolable line. Crumbling tombstones mark the graves, and scraggly cedar trees are scattered here and there, stubborn survivors of erratic prairie weather. Against the blue horizon, pink and white peony bushes bloom in random clusters, colorful spots against the brown grass.

Just east of the cemetery, I drive down a small hill and on past Reliance Dam, where my father took us fishing on Sunday afternoons. Gathering his five children around him on the grassy banks, he baited squirming earthworms on hooks, snapped red and white bobbers on the lines, and helped us maneuver the rigid bamboo poles over our heads so we could cast out toward the cattails and rushes, where he assured us schools of bullheads waited.

A few miles beyond the dam lies the south field where I took bologna sandwiches, lemonade, and spice cake to my father during his afternoon breaks from planting and cultivating the wheat. Sitting on the ground in the shade of the combine's enormous tire, knees pulled up to our chests, we'd munch on the sandwiches, our backs resting against the tire's rubber. I could hear the crows squawking overhead and the soft rattle of the dry wheat heads as the wind blew down the rows. Sometimes my father would close his eyes and take a short nap, and I'd climb the metal steps to the top of the combine and leap into the grain hopper, immersing myself in the fragrant kernels. When it was time to leave, I would fill my pockets with kernels of wheat so I could nibble on the nutty-flavored grain as I drove home.

The anticipation in the dream increases as I continue past the field, toward the gentle hill by Sunny Slope Farm, home of our nearest neighbor, and the last milestone on my journey before the final turn north to our place. When I reach that junction, the fog rolls in, enveloping the car and blocking my vision. I stop the car, get out, and stand in the middle of the road, weeping in frustration and sorrow, knowing that just on the other side of the impenetrable, gray haze waits my father. I imagine him standing in a wheat field, golden in the reflection of ripening grain that reaches his waist, his long legs spread wide and planted on the land, his hands cupped to his forehead to shade his eyes against the glare of the sun. Behind him, our small white farmhouse waits for me as well, the pink hollyhocks growing by the steps stretching nearly to the windows and the creeping jenny hugging the concrete foundation and sidewalks. I hear the soft rustling of cattle moving toward the feed bins and the hayloft's door banging in the wind, and I see the granary, its boards weathered gray, sagging to the north, an old and faithful sentry stooped by the burden of keeping watch for vagabond masters. But I can't part the haze, and I can't go home.

Time and again through the years, I awoke from that dream feeling desolate and abandoned, my face wet with tears, the now familiar pain of loss and grief as intense as the day we buried my father. I dealt with this dream for years, accepted mornings suffused with sorrow, and struggled to understand why this dream haunted me so, why it refused to let me go.

Over time, I have discovered the power of story to heal and sustain us, to provide answers to our questions, and to give us direction. As I have tried to interpret my dream, I have been especially helped by the words and stories of authors who examine the impact of landscape on personal growth. These writers have helped me understand the effects of the prairies of central South Dakota on the development of my spirit, and drawing from their wisdom, I have come to terms with my dream. I am, I now understand, what Wallace Stegner called "a 'placed' person, . . . a lover of known earth, known weather, and known neighbors, both human and inhuman." With my father's death, I suffered not only the loss of a greatly loved person but the loss of "known earth" as well. With no children willing to take over the farm, my mother had no choice but to lease and then eventually sell the land to neighbors. And so, I was abruptly separated from a significant person and place and the dream was my attempt to deal with that displacement.

Many others have written eloquently about the need to return to familiar ground. In his essay "The Brown Wasps," Loren Eiseley describes wasps returning to hives in bus stops, pigeons lured back to crumbling nests in abandoned train stations, and field mice burrowing in potted plants on patios in crowded cities. So too, says Eiseley, do humans instinctually return to places that formed or shaped them. "We cling to a time and place because without them," he wrote, "man is lost, not only man, but life."

In his book *Grassland*, Richard Manning also speaks of this need to return to familiar land, recounting the story of an elk that journeyed 1800 miles from Montana to the grasslands of Missouri. What drove this elk on this epic journey? Biologists say elk migrate for a variety of reasons, including preservation instincts, usually fleeing from hunters, and reproductive urges, particularly those which improve blood lines. However, neither motivation appeared to drive this elk's migration. During hunting season, elk typically migrate north into Canada to escape hunters, a relatively short distance for most herds. This elk moved nearly 2000 miles toward the southeast. And on his way, he passed several herds of elk, which seems to rule out reproductive urges as a motivating factor in the journey. Manning suggests that the explanation for this creature's behavior may lie in some deep, instinctual response to the grasslands of his ancestors: "It is not a great leap to believe that the grass is only a hint, a trigger of the elk's deep racial memory . . . all life is inextricably tied to the land that made it. This elk's journey was in a sense a following of the directions encoded in his genes to reclaim the land that made him." My life was a farm in central South Dakota. I lived on that farm full-time until age 6, when my father bought a house in Chamberlain, moving there for the winters because he believed that the town school district could provide a better preparation for college than could our tiny rural school. My father believed fiercely in the value of an education, "the one thing no one can take away from you," he often proclaimed. And he broadly defined education to include any lesson in something that enriched intellect or soul. To that end, he funded a variety of lessons, from piano, band, ballet, gymnastics, and baton, to the lessons inherent in books and travel. For my father, college was the pinnacle of an education, a summit he had never reached. But he vowed that his children would earn the college degree he'd never had, and the move to town was his first step in achieving this dream.

So, from the age of 6 until I was 21, I spent the school years in town and the summers on the farm; it was the best of both worlds for a child. My father farmed in partnership with his brother, and between them there were 5 sons old enough to do the fieldwork and outside chores, so I was not a farm girl who spent her days fixing fence or driving the truck to the elevator with wheat and oats during the harvest. Nor was much required from me in the house. My mother was an accomplished cook who ruled her kitchen with pride and creativity. But she was an indifferent house-keeper. And so, she expected from me only a bit of dusting now and then and the daily gathering and washing of the eggs. Many years later, as I talked with other women about growing up on a farm, I discovered how unusual my experience had been. While they remember hours of hard work, calloused hands, aching muscles, and blistering sunburns, I remember hours of solitude and leisure and immersion in the world around me.

I had the luxury of choosing from a variety of special retreats in which I might spend my days. I could take a blanket and books I'd check out from the Chamberlain Public Library and go down to the shelterbelt just north of the house to read under the plum trees. When I tired of reading, I could turn to other diversions. The shelterbelt was a haven for insects and bugs, plentiful and varied enough to provide hours of observing their colors, shapes, and habits. Dragonflies flew across my head like lilliputian helicopters, their shiny, translucent wings beating in rapid whirring motion; grasshoppers popped up from the grass leaving brown stains on my arms and legs, which my brothers claimed was tobacco juice; and fat, green worms hung from the leaves of the trees. I especially liked to watch the shiny black ground beetles. I would lie on my stomach and watch them haul small loads of dirt down and over the cracks in the dry earth, wondering what it was they were building, impressed with their industriousness and determination.

Or I could follow the reliable ruts of the cow path to the north dam and hunt for turtles and tadpoles in its muddy waters. There I would ease into the water, sinking up to my ankles in the muck, the mud oozing between my toes, the water bugs swimming around my thighs sending small bubbles to the surface. When I felt especially brave, I could sail the raft my brothers had pieced together with rotting boards from the old chicken coop, oil drums, and baling wire. Rafting across the dam presented a number of dangers, including the possibility of water snakes crawling up from under the raft to curl around my ankles and the wrath of my brothers, who thought of the raft as their private property, not to be shared with a little sister. However, most days I headed for my favorite spot on the farm, the top of the granary. Climbing to the top of the granary roof for the first time when I was 10 years old was a rite of passage for me, a passage into the world of my older brothers, who had often stood on that roof laughing down at me and my tears and my raging resentment at being grounded so ridiculously on the mundane earth while they towered over my head. Early in my childhood, I had vowed that I too would make the ascent to that high roof.

The ascent involved three steps. First, I had to climb to the top of the fence that surrounded the feedlot. From there, I stepped up to the top of the brooder house, located some three or four feet away from the granary. These two steps were fairly safe and easy. Reaching the granary roof, however, was more complicated and dangerous. This entailed standing on the brooder house with my right foot, grabbing behind the shingles of the granary with my right hand, hoisting my left leg on top of the granary roof and then quickly pulling myself up with the remaining hand. It was a dangerous proposition, but well worth the risk. I'll never forget my feeling of triumph the first time I made it to the top, after a series of failed efforts which were due largely to my fear of tumbling down into that space between the granary and the brooder house.

I was awed by the view from my place on the top of the granary. I could see for miles across the prairie, with only a handful of cottonwood trees clustered around an occasional stock pond or Medicine Butte off to the northwest breaking the line between earth and sky. I relished those long, dreamy hours by myself on the granary roof, feeling suspended in magical space between the muddy feedlot below and the wide, soft clouds above. Those hours instilled in me a love of solitude and an ease with being alone that inhabits me still. They also taught me to be intolerant of boredom. I never felt bored on that roof. I thought it wonderful to be alone high above fixed earth; wonderful to know the luxury of solitude, of fancy, and of observing my surroundings, which I always found fascinating.

Lying on the faded wooden shingles, the rough edges against my bare legs and arms, I listened to the soft, heavy breathing of the cattle in the feedlot below and the rhythmic screeching of the windmill pumping rusty, copper-scented artesian water into the cattle trough behind the barn. The musty smell of cattle manure and sweet alfalfa mixed with the clean, crisp scent of wheat piled high and drying in the grain bin below. I stashed books under the pitch of the roof, stuffing them inside Old Home bread wrappers to protect them against rain and humid summer evenings, sometimes adding oatmeal cookies and apples to my caches. I read for hours on the granary roof, stopping now and again to daydream or to watch the clouds drifting across infinite prairie sky. Unlike my older siblings, I had no gift for finding images in them. They would align my finger with a cloud and tell me it was Jimmy Durante's nose or Bugs Bunny's ears. I would concentrate on that spot as hard as I could and still see nothing but clusters, yet I marveled at the dappled-patterned shades of white, black, gray, and pink, a lace coverlet over the blue sky. Even the sky's shades of blue varied from an intense color so deep it was nearly navy to the palest, Siamese blue, the color of my father's eyes.

Mostly the granary roof was a quiet place, the sounds around me muffled by the wind across the prairie. Occasionally I heard the muted whine of a car's engine as a neighbor drove down the gravel road to the east or the dull drone of my father's tractor circling the field to the south. On rare days, I heard an airplane overhead, and I fantasized about the plane's passengers and exotic destinations. By far my favorite sound, however, was the thunderous call of Canada Geese flying overhead as they made their seasonal migration, a sound that thrilled me in large part because of my father's love for those splendid birds. In the fall, our cornfields became hospitable feeding grounds for hundreds of geese, and our stock ponds gave them respite from their flight. Each day, my father drove out to the cornfield to take the daily census of the goose population, coming home wild with excitement as the numbers grew. When he burst in the door with the latest tally, my mother rolled her eyes at us and said, "Your dad's gone giddy again, kids." And it was true; he had.

My father's giddiness over the goose numbers had little to do with the hunt. We seldom ate wild fowl at our house, except at Thanksgiving and Christmas when my mother, in a culinary concession to my father, would stuff a goose with apples and onions, wrap it in bacon, and bake it for hours to eliminate the wild taste. Perhaps he loved the geese so much because their freedom thrilled him. He was a gypsy by nature, and his youthful wanderlust led him to leave his prairie home and ride the rails with the hoboes to the 1933 Chicago World's Fair and a year later to hitchhike to the Black Hills to climb Harney Peak. Even after he planted his feet firmly in the solid ground of farm and family, he nurtured his urge to move, and at any break in the farming routine, he packed his family into our 1956 Pontiac station wagon and got moving. Or maybe, he identified with the geese because he too was part of an ancient, cyclical pattern. Like the birds' ritual spring and fall migration, he measured his years by planting and harvesting, and he must have found a familiar comfort in the certainty of the bird's routine.

My father accepted the necessity of planting and harvesting crops but found his greatest pleasure in raising and caring for livestock. Toward late afternoon each day, he would come home from the fields to tend to the cattle. I would lie on the roof, watching him stride across the yard toward the feedlot, tall and straight and elegant. He wore a wide-brimmed straw hat, a gray cotton work shirt, its sleeves buttoned at his wrists, its tail tucked into matching pants, and brown boots laced up to midcalf, protection against rattlesnakes slithering through pastures and grain fields. He moved calmly among the cluster of cattle, parting them with large hands pushed gently against their hindquarters. Although I could not distinguish the words, I could hear him murmur to the cows, calming them with his soft voice. When he reached the feeding trough, he shoveled corn into long, perfect, round rows, his strong arms straining to lift the heavy scoop shovel and dump the kernels into the troughs. His task completed, he leaned against the outside of the fence, arms resting on the top railing, hands folded as if in prayer, and watched the cattle, his face soft and tender.

On many summer days, the granary roof became my special spot for indulging in fantasy. The summer I was 10, I dreamed of being a country western singer, hearing my voice broadcast across the state on WNAX radio on the George B. German Radio Hour. "You have to practice hard if you want to be a singer," my father reminded me. And so practice I did, standing on the roof as if it were a stage, singing from deep in my belly, perfecting my talents for the cattle standing in the feedlot below. "Seeeeee them tumbling down, pledging their love to the ground," I sang, holding that first note as long as I could, like The Sons of the Pioneers. The Herefords lifted their white faces to me transfixed by my melody, and I felt empowered beyond reason by my musical talent.

One day, I decided to hypnotize a cow, having been told by my Kansas City cousin Billy that if I stared long and hard into a cow's eyes, I could have her under my control. I was excited by the prospect of putting one of our Herefords under my magic spell. Once I had her hypnotized, I could then command her to perform bizarre and wonderful tricks, better even than those I had seen at the Bewitched Village Trained Animal Show at the Reptile Gardens in the Black Hills. There, placid and obedient Guernseys stretched their long, yellow necks, clamped braided ropes between their teeth, and shook their large heads back and forth, ringing a school bell hanging over their heads. I lay flat on my stomach at the edge of the roof, pounded the shingles with my fists, and yelled "Come Boss!" until I attracted the indifferent attention of a big brown Hereford. I stared into that cow's deep brown, unflinching eyes, imagining I could make her play dead. I held back giggles as I envisioned her lying on her back, legs extended above her belly and hoofs angled to the side like a ballerina's feet in first position, while her large, rosy teats listed off to her right, resting lightly in the feedlot's mud. After staring for what seemed like hours into her eyes, my head ached and my eyes watered. And still, that cow stared back at me, never blinking, and showing no signs of submission. Finally, I gave up, forced to admit that I had been defeated by a lazy old heifer. And for some time after that, I suspected that Billy's hypnotism story was just another of his fibs, like the one he told about a black screen in a wooden box that showed moving pictures right there in their living room.

Often in late July and early August, the clouds gathered force and motion, roiling across the sky toward the farm. Then I knew that soon I would hear the gears shifting on our rusty red Chevy pickup as it roared down the driveway, my father battling with the steering wheel to keep the tires from slipping out of the deep ruts in the dirt road that led to the yard. Jammed in the front seat with my father, my older brothers would lurch in tandem with the truck. When the truck came to a spine-jarring halt, they would all pile out the doors and scatter to their designated storm responsibilities. My father would then descend into the storm cellar, sweeping through it like a soldier on night patrol, the shovel in his hand a weapon against rattlesnakes that often slept in tight coils under the shelves of canned beans and peaches. Meanwhile, my brothers would herd the cattle into the barn and battle the wide hinged doors to latch them against the wind that was blowing dust from the south field into their ex- posed faces. Watching their furious activity, I would lie flat against the pitch of the lower roof and press my body into the shingles beneath me as the wind gathered force, whooshing over the granary roof and across my back. When I would hear my mother yell, "Mary Alice, get home right now! And I mean it!!" I would climb down from the rooftop to dash sin- gle-file with my family down the narrow sidewalk to the cellar, resenting being back on the ground and tempted to challenge my mother's belief that wind was more dangerous than venomous snakes.

In general, I had the granary roof to myself. My two older brothers worked in the fields all day. My older sister, the priss, stayed indoors doing her nails and enumerating my many faults to my mother. My youngest brother, who destroyed my comfortable life as the baby of the family by being born into the family when I was five, generally knew better than to disturb me. On those rare occasions when he attempted the climb to the rooftop, I could usually scare him off by throwing pebbles I had stored for such occasions.

The summer of his 7th year, however, he grew more brazen in his efforts to invade my space, so I determined that desperate measures were needed. One day, I went down to the pasture with a shovel and a paper bag. I found a partially dry cowpie, scooped it into the bag, and carried it and the shovel up on the roof with me. Then I sat quietly waiting for my chance, my missile resting on the scoop of the shovel. Eventually, I was rewarded with the sight of Kevin's little towhead appearing level with the roof line. I let fly. Fortunately for Kevin, I miscalculated the distance, and the cowpie fell harmlessly on the shingles. But my mother found neither humor nor logic in my plan, despite the fact that Kevin emerged unsoiled. Looking back on it now, I realize that this was a mean-spirited and repugnant thing to do, but at age 12 I found it immensely satisfying. And it was a moment that taught me one of the many lessons of my childhood: sometimes you have to protect your own turf, especially turf that provides you respite, a sense of belonging, and an opportunity to grow into yourself. "A man has a right to his place," said Eisely.

I know now that another lesson space and prairie instilled in me was a keen sense of my place in this world. Although many people believe rural folk lead narrow and provincial lives, I argue that the opposite is true. Urban children look out their windows to a world only as wide as the streets outside their homes, their view limited by houses or apartment buildings. From my roof, I saw an endless horizon, an unobstructed perspective that taught me that my world was only a small part of a much larger one.

In his book *The Blue Bird Sings to the Lemonade Springs*, Wallace Stegner writes about the impact of space on the psyche of prairie people. He says: ". . . there is something about living in big, empty space, where people are few and distant, under a great sky that is alternately serene and furious, exposed to sun from four in the morning till nine at night, and to a wind that never seems to rest—there is some-thing about exposure to that country that not only tells an individual how small he is, but steadily who he is."

Stegner's words resonate for me. The landscape I could see from my granary rooftop helped me to know myself and to keep myself in perspective. The expansiveness of sky and prairie forced me to realize that my existence is not really all that important beyond my circle of family and friends. I am neither depressed nor discouraged by the awareness that I am comparatively insignificant; rather, I find it liberating. Knowing this frees me from taking myself too seriously, from feeling the burden of responsibility for people and situations over which I have no control.

Lois Hudson also discusses the impact the prairie had on her maturation. She says, ". . . I was raised on the prairies and my world was a world of elements, not of streets and houses, and a world of myself, not of other peoples' explanations of myself. . . ." That, too, speaks to my experience. The isolation of our prairie home offered me the luxury of living in a world of myself, of determining who I was long before I was forced to deal with other people's ideas about me. That taught me not to look to others for affirmation, but rather to find it within myself. That is not to say that I do not look at myself critically and realistically; I can be very candid about my faults. But I do not expect others to make me feel good about myself, nor am I much affected by criticism that I believe to be unfair. That may be the most valuable lesson I learned from the prairie and from the hours of solitude that allowed me to become comfortable with who I am. Others cannot make you happy. That must come from within.

As much as I identify myself with the prairie of Lyman County, I know with certainty that I will never return to stay. It is the poignant irony of my father's life that in his determined effort to educate his children, to prepare us to participate in a world beyond the farm, a world the Depression had closed to him; in working so hard to give us that world, he dislodged us forever from his own. As my brother Kevin once wrote, "For all his talent for growing things, he couldn't raise one farmer. Not one."

Over the years, the buildings on the farm began to deteriorate, victims of neglect and misuse. We kept track of the damage through rumors reported to us, periodic tales of loss and devastation. One August we heard that a violent tornado had swept through the county the night before, hitting our barn with such force that it collapsed inward, leaving the doors, rafters and boards lying in heaps in the stalls where our cattle once stood. Sometime later we were told that the south wall of the granary had caved in, its shingles and support beams filling up the granary bins below. An especially painful story came from old neighbors, who said that they had seen a light shining late one night from our place. The next morning when one of the neighbors went to investigate, he found the ruins of a keg party thrown by kids who'd discovered the empty house. By all accounts, it was a wild night. To gain access to the house, they had kicked open the door to the front porch and left it lying on the floor, a gaping hole in its middle the evidence of someone's boot. Inside the house, they had littered the floors with broken beer bottles, shattered glass, and cigarette butts. They had spray painted obscenities on the walls and torn down the curtains, piling them in heaps in the corners. We felt violated and sad and haunted by the image of drunken kids staggering through our rooms, tracking mud across the kitchen linoleum, leaving dirty handprints on the floral wall-paper in the living room, sullying our bedrooms, our most private of spaces.

One day, the new owners flooded the ruins with gas, threw a match to the rubble, and set it on fire, leaving the visible remains of my past in ashes. When I heard that that the buildings had been burned, I was surprised by the grief that I felt, for I believed that I had long before come to terms with the loss of the farm and the accompanying pain of that loss. I thought of the ashes left by the fire and how prairie winds would carry them away and summer rains and winter snows would soak them into the soil until the ashes became the land itself. And in the end, I thought, not even ashes remain; there is nothing left, nothing like a roadside marker which says:

"On this spot once lived a man and a woman and their five children. For 30 years this family forged a life based on faith in the land, the seasons, and the future. Take notice as you pass by."

And then one clear autumn day as I walked with my husband down a gravel road not far from our house, I heard the dry rustling leaves of a cottonwood tree, a sound that struck me with the force of recognition. And I thought of the many hours I had played beneath the cottonwood trees on the north dam, had watched the soft cotton fall around me like snow, had gathered it in my hands and carried it back to my room to make beds for my paper dolls. And I said to him, "I remember when . . .", and I began to tell the story of the cottonwood trees, and the north dam and the garter snakes and toads I hunted in its muddy water, and of the raft I sailed on a body of water that seemed like an ocean to a small girl. And as I told my story, I realized that the buildings had not been the monument to my life on that place after all, for it is story that preserves life, ensures that the past has a place in the future. And my story is in those cottonwood trees and the plum trees in the shelterbelt, and in the insects that crawl over cracked earth and in the birds that cry overhead, and in the soft sighing of the prairie grass as the wind blows across it, and in the billowing white clouds that move across the vast expanse of blue prairie sky. The story of my place is the story of that which is timeless.

Today, my dream no longer haunts me, and I do not drive the back roads in search of my father, for I now know that he is always with me. I see him in brown Hereford cattle grazing in tall, prairie grass, lifting their snowy faces expectantly as I pass by.

I know him in ripe, golden wheat fields and in the churning dust from a combine as it moves through the rows of grain. I feel him in the migrating goose as it rises from the water and stretches its long, elegant neck into the wind, its wide, powerful wings pulsing a steady, efficient rhythm, its deep, determined eyes focused on the journey ahead.

Discussion Questions:

1. In this essay, the writer describes a sacred place in her life. What place is sacred to you and why? Are sacred places still important or even possible today?

2. In "Landscape and Narrative," Barry Lopez wrote, ". . . the shape of the individual mind is affected by land as it is by genes." What does he mean by this? Have you been shaped by landscape?

3. Many writers have written about land. What is one of the best landscape stories you have ever read? What was so striking about this story?

4. This essay is a narrative of loss and recovery. What has the writer lost and what has she recovered? What made the recovery possible for her?

Frogs

Joe Paddock

From a story told by Delmar Debbaut

At that time there was still a pothole
over every hill and the frogs in the fall
swarmed like maggots in the carcass of a
dead horse.
Sometimes, after the coming of the cars,
they had to get out the blade to scrape the slick
of crushed frogs off that road that circles
Stork Lake.

One sunny Saturday afternoon in late September,
more than forty years back now,
down around the bay,
about fifteen town kids began to herd frogs
up from the water's edge where they lay
dozing in the sun by the thousands,
big heavy leopard frogs that would stretch
nine, ten inches from nose to toe claw.

They herded them slowly
up over Anderson's pasture hill.
You would've thought it was wind through grass
sweeping ahead of them.

Herded them up onto the road into town,
herded them with real care, losing a few here
    and there,
but maintaining the mass
(some guessed five thousand, some ten),
and at the corner of Sixth,
they turned them, losing maybe forty dozen
which bounced on over Hershey's lawn,
confusing the bejesus out of their old Basset
    hound, Monty,
who, after sniffing and poking with his paw,
sat down and howled at a thin silver sliver
    of day moon
in the sky.

Old Mrs. Angier said she first heard a sound
like five thousand hands patting meat,
and when she looked up the street, she saw
these kids, serious and quiet, with a grey-brown
    wave,
like swamp water to their knees,
rolling along in front of them.

Mrs. Angier said, "Now, you never heard a word
from a single one of those kids.
They were silent and strange with that haze of a wave
rolling along in front of them.
Just that patting sound
times five thousand.
I tell you, it made goose flesh roll
up my back and arms!"

The boys claimed later that they had no plan,
but, when they came alongside "Horse" Nelson's
Fixit Quick Garage—which contained

maybe a half dozen broken-down cars
and "Horse" and Allen, his son, and "Windy"
      Jeffers—
one kid barked: "Bring 'em on in!"
and they turned that herd of frogs on a dime
(they were herding easy by that time),
and ran them through the entranceway.
Young Jim Hedeen grabbed the handle
of the sliding door and rolled her shut,
and those kids vanished like fifteen rabbits
into whatever weed patch they could find.

Well, hell, you can imagine.
"Windy" was on his back working upward on a
      spring
when those slimy devils started sliding all
      over him.
They say he most-near tipped that Model A
      on its side
getting out of there. And "Horse,"
who was no doubt nearly through his daily pint
of peach brandy, dropped a cam shaft
on Allen's toe and ran and hid in the can,
and Allen, who'd been mean and noisy
from his first squawk on, began hopping
      one-footed
amidst that froth of frogs. (And you know
how they have a way of climbing
up the inside of your pants, all wet
and with those scratchy little claws!)
Allen, slam-banging whatever came to hand,
tipped a couple cars from jacks, and screamed:
"I'M GONNA GET KEVIN KLIMSTRA FOR THIS!"

Forty-three years have passed,
but those frogs have never quit rolling
from the tongues of people around town.
It's one of those stories you learn early
and carry with you, and measure
the taste of life by
till the day you die.

Discussion Questions:

1. How does humor affect relationship?

2. Why does individual memory sometimes differ from what might be called "collective memory"?

3. How might collective memory detract from or contribute to community?

4. What is a true story?

Clear Lake, South Dakota During the Great Depression and World War II: A Case Study in Community

John E. Miller

In their discussions of community, sociologists focus on face-to-face relationships in places where people know each other well and on the reciprocity that guides their personal dealings with each other. German Sociologist Ferdinand Tonnies usefully contrasted the tight-knit communal relationships that characterized small villages and rural areas in preindustrial Europe with the looser, more anonymous kinds of interactions that became more common when increasing numbers of people moved into cities and began to work in factories and offices and live in apartments and urban housing developments.[1] Something important was lost in the process, he suggested: intimacy, predictability, stability, and a sense of security. But something was also gained, he thought: greater freedom, openness, diversity, and a willingness to experiment and deviate from the norm.

Americans have always been conflicted between their longing for community and their desire for personal freedom. The great French social commentator Alexis de Tocqueville, in his classic analysis *Democracy in America*, depicted the continual tension in American culture between individualism and community.[2] Throughout our history, the pendulum has continually swung back and forth between efforts to achieve greater freedom and individualism, on the one hand, and greater cooperation and community, on the other.

This essay endeavors to describe change and continuity in community life in a typical small town on the edge of the prairie and plains during the Great Depression and World War II. It aims to provide a benchmark for discussing how community has evolved in small towns in recent decades. Clear Lake, South Dakota, was a typical county seat town with a population around 800 when the Stock Market Crash shattered America's old way of life in October of 1929. A little less than fifty years old at the time, Clear Lake, named for a small lake directly east of it, had been established as an agricultural marketing town along the Burlington, Cedar Rapids, and Northern Railroad in the midst of the Great Dakota Boom of the early 1880s. In little more than five years' time, most of eastern South Dakota filled up with ambitious homesteaders and energetic townspeople, eager to make a living off the fruits of the land.[3]

As was the case in many neighboring communities, Clear Lake's population ranked high in people with German, Norwegian, and other Scandinavian backgrounds and in native-born Americans who had migrated across the northern tier of states from New England and New York. Almost no one came from states south of the Mason and Dixon line or from countries in eastern and southern Europe.[4] Many families who located in the town and surrounding agricultural precincts during the 1880s had stopped over in one or more places in the Midwest before migrating to Dakota Territory (it became South Dakota after 1889), and some stayed only temporarily before moving further west or backtracking east.[5]

With population origins like these, the kinds of church groups that established themselves in Clear Lake were predictable. The six groups in town in 1929 were the Congregational, Methodist Episcopal, First Baptist, St. Paul's Lutheran (Norwegian), Zion Evangelical (German), and St. Mary's Catholic parish. Three years later, Trinity Lutheran was founded to serve Wisconsin Synod parishioners, and over the years several other congregations emerged and several disappeared. These churches were highly visible and influential in the community. One or more pastors was always present to offer invocations and benedictions at Memorial Day services, Armistice Day observances, high school graduation ceremonies, and other events. Baccalaureate services were an integral part of the graduation week schedule. The local newspaper regularly listed the churches' weekly schedules and carried news of ladies' aids and youth group events. At Easter and Christmas, the front page of the paper often was largely taken over by church programs or sermonettes.

The Catholic parish consisted of a small group of about twenty-five mostly Irish families. Organized religion in Clear Lake was pervasively Protestant. With the exception of the Lutherans, who remained more committed to doctrinal purity than the others, the various Protestant congregations paid little heed to denominational distinctions. "Union services," involving an exchange of pastors and joint worship, were common, especially at Thanksgiving time. Special evangelism services and weeklong revival meetings frequently united Congregationalists, Methodists, Baptists, and Evangelicals in worship.

Pastors from the four Protestant groups also joined in establishing a Ministerial Association (again without the Lutherans). The group waxed and waned, depending on the ministers who were involved in it. The churches were a pervasive presence in the community and some people, at least, considered the town to be much above average in its religious involvement ("Clear Lake Claims Champion Church City of the World," touted a front-page article in the local weekly newspaper.[6]) But the town probably differed little from its counterparts in its mix of piety and backsliding. An interesting survey of the community in 1940 revealed that only 33 per cent of the population attended services regularly, while 47 per cent never went to church.[7]

No less important than the church in community life was the school. Not everyone was a church member, but everyone went to school—most through the eighth grade at least. With approximately twenty-five students in each of the lower eight grades, Clear Lake Grade School's enrollment ranged between 170 and 200 in a typical year. High school enrollments, fed by graduates from Clear Lake and surrounding towns and from more than a dozen rural schools in the area, varied more widely, with graduating classes ranging between twenty and thirty-five. Overall, elementary enrollments in the county, as was true all over the state, declined during the Depression decade by a little more than ten per cent, while high school enrollments increased by close to a third.[8] Like schools everywhere, Clear Lake's focused on the basics, although the curriculum began to expand with the introduction of home economics and shop classes during the 1920s.

As was also true everywhere, organizational activities proliferated during the decade after World War I. All the town grade schools and every country school set up Young Citizens Leagues to promote citizenship, knowledge of parliamentary procedure, and participation in school and community betterment projects. Music became more important. By the early thirties, as many as 400 students from the eight town schools in the county joined in a large all-day music festival in Clear Lake.[9] High school students, too, had an increasing variety of musical activities available to them, including a school band, organized in 1930, and choral groups, which competed in interscholastic competitions. Each year, the juniors put on a class play, as did the seniors, during graduation week.

Interscholastic athletics also grew to larger proportions during the twenties and thirties, as schools adopted nicknames (Clear Lake's was the Cardinals) and established athletic conferences with nearby schools. In 1940, Clear Lake joined a new football conference, called the State Line Six-Man Football Conference, which also included Elkton, Gary, and White.[10] Its basketball team ranged farther afield, playing teams from Gary, Clark, Astoria, Estelline, White, Brookings, Canby, Minnesota, and other towns.

As schools became increasingly sports and activity-minded, educational achievement inevitably lost a little of its primacy as a goal. Schools had never been exclusively educational in intent. They had always served as key players in the socialization process. Citizenship classes retained a place in the curriculum, but they were not the only place where values were taught. Each week, for example, third graders were given a poem to memorize, not only to improve their memorization skills and to enhance their aesthetic appreciation, but also to improve their characters.

70

One such verse in November 1929 went:

The world is such a happy place
That children, whether big or small,
Should always have a smiling face
And never, never sulk at all.

A couple of years later, the motto on the board for the week was: There are two rules which ought to be written on every heart: never believe anything bad about anybody unless you positively know that it is true; never tell even that unless you feel that it is absolutely necessary and that God is listening to you tell it.

By such poems, mottos, stories, and lessons, students in third grade and in all of the grades learned not only Reading, Writing, and Arithmetic, but also how to be kind, considerate, helpful, and useful. Each year, the state of South Dakota conducted Character Training Institutes to improve the teaching of ethical principles in the schools. In 1936, County School Superintendent Maria Holen noted the many types of organized activities—both inside and outside the schools—that served to promote character education among young people: the Young Citizens League, 4-H clubs, Boy and Girl Scout Troops, Parent-Teacher Associations, and Sunday Schools.[11] All of these groups were active in Clear Lake and in the rest of Deuel County.

It was not only though the schools and other organized activities, however, that the community operated to socialize the young and to establish social control. The third central social institution (in addition to church and school) was the home. Primary responsibility for training and educating children remained in parents' hands, but friends, neighbors, and kin did not hesitate to intervene in looking out for and disciplining children. If a neighbor's child or someone from outside the neighborhood was misbehaving, adults felt obliged to get involved and set the child straight or to inform the parent or guardian about what had happened. In May, 1933, newspaper editor A. G. Warner related an episode in which a group of small boys got into trouble for breaking into a slot machine and taking the pennies. "When called on the carpet and given a lecture, they expressed regret and promised not to repeat such an act," the editor reported. "If these boys only knew how anxious everybody is that they behave themselves, we believe they would never do wrong."[12]

"Anxious" was certainly the correct word to have used, for no doubt there were plenty of young boys in town who sometimes veered away from the good and the true, which meant that there were adults, too, who did not conform to approved norms. It was no wonder that when circus acts and carnivals came to town, spokesmen organizing the festivities advertised the acts as "clean and wholesome" or that newspaper editors took pleasure in reporting that when large crowds were in town for some event, there was "surprisingly little rowdiness displayed."[13] Such observations would have been unnecessary had not impolite behavior been a real threat to community tranquility. Halloween was one day in the year when some of the restraints could be abandoned and the boys and young men of the town were allowed to have some fun overturning outhouses and setting machinery on top of buildings. But there were limits. When the "boys" got a little too energetic in soaping and greasing store windows on October 31 and also broke windows in an old woman's home, the newspaper editor took them to task and called for an end to such rowdy behavior.

Community during the 1930s was inclusive; regardless of age, sex, social class, race, or religious denomination, everyone was expected to participate and all were expected to conform to social dictates. With such a homogeneous population (few Irish, few Catholics, almost no Southern and Eastern Europeans, and virtually no blacks or Jews), the population was not often tested regarding its tolerance for other lifestyles or unorthodox beliefs. Local leaders' reaction to the rise of the Farm Holiday movement during the Great Depression, however, provides a clue to the limits of their tolerance. The Farm Holiday became active in the state in 1932 with efforts to boycott the shipping of agricultural products to market as a means of bringing about higher farm prices. The main activity of the organization in Deuel County in the fall of 1933 appears to have been organized by men coming across the border from Minnesota, where the movement was better organized and more militant than it was in South Dakota. Community leaders in Clear Lake and elsewhere organized a Law and Order League in opposition to the strike, denouncing the violence they associated with boycott activity and promising to oppose further strike action. In the wake of these moves, the strike dissipated.[14]

Generally, the community avoided overt conflict between groups. It sought to promote and reinforce its values, not through violence or force, but through countless daily interactions. People modeled their behavior to set examples for others, engaging in activities that publicized and reinforced community norms and participating in rituals and celebrations. Of the latter, while Christmas and Thanksgiving were much anticipated and eagerly celebrated each year, the most significant days of the year from the point of view of cementing social ties and reinforcing a sense of community were probably Memorial Day and the Fourth of July. Each exalted nationalism and patriotism; each celebrated important values such as duty, honor, and sacrifice; and each bound people together in a display of unity and togetherness.

July 4 was not celebrated every year in towns like Clear Lake, but Memorial Day ceremonies were always conducted. Usually held on the courthouse lawn, the Memorial Day program began with an invocation by a local pastor and ended with a benediction. In between came the Veterans' Roll Call and a patriotic address, plus several musical selections by choral groups, soloists, or a band, with the audience invited to join in on "America" and "The Star Spangled Banner." Sometimes the Gettysburg Address was recited. Afterwards, many of the assembled would join in a parade to the cemetery, where graves of fallen soldiers would be decorated with flowers. All was conducted with solemn dignity, as befitted the day.

The Fourth of July was a different kind of occasion, full of merriment and fun. Most businesses closed for it, as they did for Memorial Day.[15] Often, people went to another town to join in its celebration or to a nearby lake, such as Cochrane, Kampeska, Big Stone, Pickerel, or Enemy

Swim. The 1936 program in Clear Lake, typical of the event, began with a ten o'clock parade down Main Street (with appropriate prizes awarded for best floats and entries), followed by a dinner at noon and a concert by the band of La Bolt, a town in nearby Grant County. In the afternoon, prizes of several dollars each were awarded for winners of bicycle, horse, and pony races and a half-mile dash. These events were followed by a baseball game between Clear Lake and Toronto, with a cash prize awarded to the winning team. On the street in the evening were another band concert and a variety of running races for kids and adults of all ages, along with a dance at the Ford Garage. Climaxing the day's events was a fireworks display.[16]

Through the years, patriotic remembrance on these days increasingly gave way to personal pleasure and entertainment, causing newspaper editors to chide the public for its lackadaisical attitude and for forgetting the original purpose of the ceremonies. In 1941, just six months before Pearl Harbor, editor Ted Burges of the *Courier-Advocate* lamented the many empty seats at the Memorial Day exercises—a sign, he said, of people's lax patriotism and lack of gratefulness for the sacrifices of the soldiers being honored. The day should have had deep meaning for every American, the editor observed, but there were too many who used the day as "a convenient excuse to engage in some form of recreation or a day of rest from all-night celebration which usually occurs on the night before a holiday."[17]

Most days of the year were not invested with as much meaning as holidays and the Sabbath. Most days were ordinary, routine, filled with work, attending school, visiting with friends, relaxing, eating, sleeping, existing from one moment to the next. However, once the day's work and routine tasks were out of the way, people often got together informally in twos, threes, and small groups. They also participated in a multitude of organizations bringing larger groups—usually a dozen or two, but sometimes many more—together to achieve designated goals or simply for enjoyment.

Segregation by gender remained prevalent until after World War II. Most of the religious denominations had ladies' aids with high and worthy purposes, such as foreign missions or the study of Scripture, but they never waited too long to bring out the "dainty refreshments" or "tasty lunch" or whatever the newspaper editor chose to call them in his paragraph items on the locals page of the paper. While they were sometimes held in the church parlors, these meetings usually took place in people's homes, which effectively limited them to women whose husbands earned enough of an income for them to feel comfortable inviting a dozen or more of their friends in for discussion and food.

In addition to their usual bimonthly meetings (often discontinued during the warm months of summer), the ladies' aids put on dinners, suppers, ice cream socials, and other money-raisers, along with bazaars featuring embroidery and fancy work and other handmade items or things from their gardens. Everything from fried chicken and homemade sausage to waffles and bean soup made up the menus at these affairs. At a typical gathering in 1929, the Norwegian Lutheran Ladies Aid served meat loaf, scalloped potatoes, beans, bread, buns, lefse, cake, and pies. Their Methodist counterparts five years later served a traditional New England dinner, featuring baked beans, brown bread, and "all accessories." Sometimes these meals were served in a lodge hall, a business building, or some other place, but usually they took place in church basements, making them some of the most important sites for nurturing community in town.

Women also had their counterparts to the various male fraternal organizations. The Order of Eastern Star met at the Masonic Lodge Hall on Tuesday nights, while the Royal Neighbors of America, associated with the International Order of Odd Fellows, met in the R.N.A. Hall over a clothing store. There were also a Rebekah Lodge and units of the Women's Christian Temperance Union and the American Legion Auxiliary. The Women's Federated Study Club met regularly to investigate subjects such as "Modern Trends in Education." In addition, there were several Home Extension Clubs in and around Clear Lake. Bridge was popular, and there was a club—the Brigidaires—for it. Other card games like pinochle and Grand Nula had their own clubs while they were faddish. Some of the younger women in town found enjoyment in playing "kittenball" games with competitors from other communities.

Lacking the kind of gender-based religious organizations corresponding to the ladies' aids, men found outlets for their energies in a variety of recreational activities, from baseball and golf to hunting and fishing. Increasingly, they spent their time being spectators at games played by town teams and high school teams. Baseball, the national game, enjoyed a large following in Clear Lake, as it did in most small towns. Younger children played catch and pick-up games in backyards and vacant lots. Some years, the Clear Lake American Legion Post sponsored a junior baseball team (American Legion baseball was born in 1925 in Milbank, 30 miles to the northeast). Baseball games with other towns, sometimes with purses for the winning teams, frequently drew large crowds at Fourth of July celebrations, county fairs, and summer picnics. Informal games pitting married men against single men or other matchups provided local wags with something to talk about for days afterwards. A new lighted field was installed at the city park on the north end of town in 1933. Sometimes benefit dances or other fundraisers would be held to provide financial support for town teams. During the late thirties, Clear Lake competed in an eight-team Eastern Dakota League along with Toronto, Dempsey, Lake Norden, Estelline, Brandt, Castlewood, and a team sponsored by Al's Service. Baseball continued to be played during the war years, and by 1945 the locals were part of a new league that included Gary, La Bolt, Bemis, Brandt, and Antelope Valley.

More men found their recreational outlet in hunting and fishing. The many lakes in the surrounding region drew anglers from miles around. Cars packed with fishermen and their gear regularly headed to the lakes to get their limits. Big Stone Lake, to the northeast along the Minnesota border, was especially popular, but Lake Cochrane, Clear Lake, and other bodies of water beckoned too. By September and October, fishing poles gave way to shotguns, as hunters criss-crossed nearby fields and wetlands in quest of pheasants, grouse, ducks, geese, and other fowl. These activities, while not operating in the same organized fashion as baseball teams and other formal groups, provided a major amount of social activity for men and contributed significantly to the sense of community in Clear Lake.

Golf, which arrived during the 1920s, got some mentions in the local paper, but seems not to have been as popular a sport in Clear Lake as it was in other places. One kind of competition that garnered considerable publicity for Clear Lake was corn husking, and contests were held every October, with winners in the county contest proceeding to the state level and occasionally to the national level. In 1937, Chance Stone won the state contest by picking 16.02 bushels of corn in 80 minutes (with deductions for gleanings), qualifying him for the national contest in a farmer's field near Marshall, Missouri, where he finished sixth in the competition. Stone demonstrated that his victory had been no fluke, repeating as county champion in 1939 and capturing the state title again the following year.[18]

Something new on the scene in 1940 was the formation of a bowling league, made possible by the construction on Main Street of a bowling alley, which contained four modern Brunswick lanes equipped with automatic pin-spotters.[19] In short order, a bowling league was formed, and several dozen men and women joined up. World War II did nothing to slow down league play. Within two years' time, there were ten teams in the men's league and six in the women's. By the end of the war there were eighteen teams operating. Results of matches were reported weekly in the paper. With five players on each team, the ninety players involved in league play constituted a significant fraction of the adult population of the town (some, no doubt, drove in from out of town). Most of their averages were in the 130s and 140s.[20] Participation in the bowling league was just one indication of the high level of organization and community activity in Clear Lake during this time.

During the decades after the Civil War, one of the most distinctive features of American culture was the pervasiveness of men's fraternal organizations, which, in turn, spawned their women's counterparts. In small towns like Clear Lake between the Civil War and World War II, to be a Main Street storekeeper, a professional, or a businessman meant almost automatically that one became a lodge member. Some men would be out several nights a week attending lodge meetings. These groups served a variety of functions—recreational, business, political, and social. At a time before movies, radio, and television, attending lodge meetings was a mode of relaxation for men that also satisfied their need for sociability. Males bonded in a variety of ways, just as their female counterparts did.

Clear Lake did not have as many fraternal groups as some small towns did, but it had its fair share. Most important was the A.F. & A.M. Masonic Lodge #129, which met on Monday nights. After 1931, these meetings were held in the old Clear Lake Opera House, which was converted into a Masonic Temple when the Majestic Theatre was built for showing movies.[21] At the start of each new year, it was time for the joint installation of officers for the Masons and the Order of Eastern Star (Ruth Chapter #50). Many husbands and wives were members of these two organizations. The Odd Fellows had their own hall and also met on Monday nights. Something new after World War I was the appearance of two new veterans organizations—the American Legion and the Veterans of Foreign Wars, which reorganized in 1936. The wives of the members of the Charles Curry Post #40 of the American Legion had their own American Legion Auxiliary unit.

In 1930, the Lions Club International organized a chapter in Clear Lake, consisting primarily of local businessmen. In addition to providing relaxation and camaraderie, their bimonthly meetings did serious business in regard to promoting the community. The booster spirit was pervasive in small-town America, but maintaining it at a high level was often a chore. Optimism and high aspiration often gave way to despondency and self-doubt and just plain lethargy and inertia, because the farm economy remained unstable, population stability remained precarious, businesses disappeared, and people resisted getting involved. The goals of the Lions included promoting good principles and citizenship, improving the business climate, taking an active interest in civic affairs, and enhancing the moral welfare of the community. The club promoted an activist, patriotic, booster spirit. It sponsored a 4-H Corn Club for rural boys, took the initiative in getting the principal streets of the town graveled, agitated for getting a new train depot built, worked to have the lake dredged, put up additional street lighting for Christmas displays, distributed hundreds of sacks of nuts and candy to children at Christmastime, and engaged in a wide variety of other projects that enhanced the quality of life in the community.

In 1936, a Commercial Club, whose membership overlapped with that of the Lions, was established to accomplish similar ends. As was often true in other towns, these kinds of groups waxed and waned over time, relying upon the initiative of a small core of leaders to keep the fires lighted under the general membership to get things done. A major move, foreshadowing the future, came in February, 1944 when at the Commercial Club's annual meeting, held in the basement of St. Paul's Lutheran Church, the seventy-five members present talked about securing a hospital for Clear Lake.[22]

As the Great Depression gave way to improved economic times and as war shadows gathered on the horizon during the late 1930s, Clear Lake's leaders took a number of steps to bring about change and stimulate business activity in town. In June, 1940 they organized the first annual Hey Days, a tradition that continued on into the war years. Billing it as Clear Lake's businessmen's gift to the people in their local trade territory, the two-day event provided a variety of attractions—free stage shows, musical performances, comedians, magicians, and more than a dozen "clean side shows." The Art B. Thomas Shows alternated with Jay Gould's Million Dollar Shows and Circus in providing the entertainment, probably depending on the schedules of those groups as they traveled from town to town in the region during the summer. Reporting on the 1941 extravaganza, the local paper estimated that the crowds roaming the streets of Clear Lake constituted the largest assemblage of humanity in the history of the town, with people coming from as far as fifty miles away to take in the games and fun.[23]

Main Street businessmen understood better than most in the community that the economic health of small towns like Clear Lake resulted largely from their ability to persuade their own people to shop at home and to attract people from other places to come and conduct their business there. Increasing automobile ownership and constantly improving vehicles along with better and faster roads created opportunities as well as dangers for small towns. For those able to attract customers from longer distances, profits could soar; for those whose earlier customers now drove to other towns, the outlook turned bleak. Main Street store-owners tried to get the stay-home-to-shop message across to people in their own community by placing newspaper ads, conducting special sales, and talking it up with their fellow townspeople.[24]

Clear Lake experienced considerable change during the 1930s and early 1940s, but it was easy enough for people to deny the signs of it and to believe that life would go on as it always had. The construction in 1930 of the Majestic Theatre, which advertised itself as being "modern in every respect," ushered in the age of the "talkies," and now moviegoers could take in as many as three or four different shows a week.[25] Sometimes the bill changed five times in a single week. Now, instead of appearing at the opera house, the school auditorium, or the courtroom of the courthouse, visiting political dignitaries were more likely to speak at the Majestic. When Governor Tom Berry came to town in October, 1934, the crowd was standing room only.[26]

Nine miles north of town, where Highway 77 intersected with Highway 212 at Tunerville, the Prairie Moon Ball Room opened in 1938, providing another distraction and pulling people away from Clear Lake. Hundreds of people came out to dance and—it was rumored—to drink, especially when bands with big reputations throughout the area provided the music. Radio was another distraction, and by the 1930s most homes had one. With musical and entertainment programs increasingly bombarding their senses, Clear Lake's residents saw less to entice them in local talent performances and homemade entertainment. The fourth annual stunt night featuring acts and performances by local people, at the Majestic Theatre in October, 1931, was the last one reported in the paper.[27] Apparently, these kinds of community gatherings were losing their appeal.

However, one activity that remained a reminder of the slower, quieter days of the past continued strong long into the forties and fifties: the old-time Saturday Night. Saturday night in small-town America between the wars and continuing on for a decade or so afterwards provided the quintessential community experience in the Midwest. Nothing else could match it in numbers of people involved, psychological investment, and the variety of social groups represented.

Traditional small towns were not perfect, by any means. There were conflicts aplenty in most of them. Petty squabbles, social ostracism, family feuds, cheating, lying, intolerance, and bigotry were not uncommon. But face-to-face interactions were the norm. People knew who you were and what you were. They looked you in the eye and they usually looked out for you. The spirit of community manifested itself it in a wide variety of ways, as is evident from the high degree of organized and informal social activities described here. Americans clung to notions of freedom and individual responsibility, but the pull of community remained strong.

World War II further reinforced community ties, even as dozens of young men left for military training camps and many others traveled to the West Cost and elsewhere to take jobs in war factories and other businesses. In a way that even the Depression failed to do, the challenges posed by military conflict forced everyone to contribute to the community's welfare and survival. "There isn't a single privileged character among us," observed Ted Burges in the *Courier-Advocate* two months after Pearl Harbor. "The war affects everyone and the sooner we realize that fact the better it will be. To fail in this war on the home front as well as on the military, would be death for free enterprise, death for free government, death for all the freedoms."[28]

Everyone, regardless of age, gender, occupation, social status, educational attainment, or physical ability, could contribute to the war effort; no one could escape the obligation to participate. War bond drives, price ceilings, food and gasoline rationing, scrap metal and rubber drives, paper drives, vehicular speed limits, rising income taxes, V-mail, even a blackout or two: all got people involved in the war effort. Every couple of weeks, as new batches of recruits boarded trains heading for Fort Snelling to begin their military training, crowds of townspeople gathered at the depot to send them off. Service flags with blue stars for the families' servicemen hung in windows. As the war ground on, the front page of the newspaper regularly ran the pictures of servicemen killed in action, and the blue stars were replaced by gold ones. Two of the front page's seven columns were devoted every week to news and pictures about the war and to letters written by men in the service. The Majestic Theatre showed movies like "Doughboys in Ireland" and "Salute to the Marines." The war, as was true everywhere else, was ubiquitous.

But even in the midst of war, total commitment to community goals and values did not occur. There were newspaper stories noting only partial subscriptions to war bond quotas and urging people to dig deeper into their pockets; there were complaints from people about rationing and price-fixing; and there were suggestions that some people were profiting excessively from wartime conditions. According to a local newspaper story, filling stations were besieged, selling five to ten times as much gasoline as usual right before rationing went into effect, as dozens of vehicles filled up their tanks and even brought along five- and ten-gallon containers to fill before ration stamps were required.

However, most people were willing to do their duty if it was made clear to them what they should do and how it could be accomplished. Farm Security Administration officials urged farmers to avoid new purchases of machinery and implements by sharing equipment with neighbors. Even grade school and high school students could play a useful role in the war by buying war stamps at school, participating in paper and scrap drives, and collecting milkweed pods for life preservers. Women's Extension Clubs studied ways to make economical wartime meals, substituting for scarce items and conserving on food where they could.

The big boost given to the economy by wartime spending made all of this more palatable. Farm prices soared and tenancy significantly decreased. Farmers began paying down their debts and buying more tractors and machinery. Unemployment became a thing of the past, and cash registers were busy. Now the biggest economic problem was a labor shortage. Like businessmen in towns all around, those in Clear Lake volunteered to go out into the fields to help local farmers bring in the harvest. Besides the many new ways in which community life was strengthened by the war, old connections and activities carried over in new ways as well. Continuity, rather than change, was the watchword with regard both to the organizational and to the informal realms. High school athletic competition continued, as did dances at Tunerville and the county fair. Church ladies' aid societies continued to meet and the Lions Club and most organizations carried on as before. Hey Days remained as popular as ever, and people drove from as far as fifty miles in 1943, despite gas rationing. Prospects for the community looked bright, and, anticipating the end of the war, people could justifiably believe that Clear Lake's future would be a continuation of trends already in place. They could think that their destiny was in their own hands and that they could— through hard work, grit, determination, and a little bit of creativity— make their own history.

For a while during the late 1940s and 1950s, a sense of optimism prevailed. But by the 1960s, social and economic forces destructive of community were becoming increasingly evident, and towns like Clear Lake found themselves on the defensive. They appeared to be caught up in the kinds of trends that journalists and academics of the time saw contributing to mass society, social alienation, and the loss of individualism. But history has a way of surprising people. It is more complex, fraught with contradictions, and unpredictable than many would admit. Just as athletes have to play the game before the outcome can become known, people, in their everyday lives, possess opportunities to affect their own history. Clear Lake would demonstrate its resiliency and creativity in adapting to change during the decades after World War II. The spirit of community would endure, although not without modifications, in the town.

Notes:

1. Ferdinand Toennies, *Community and Society*, trans. Charles P. Loomis (1887, reprint East Lansing: Michigan State University Press, 1957).

2. Alexis de Tocqueville, *Democracy in America*, trans. George Lawrence, ed. J.P. Mayer (New York: Doubleday, Anchor Books, 1969).

3. For the history of Clear Lake, see Clear Lake Centennial History Book Committee, *A Precious Legacy: Clear Lake, 1884-1984* (Clear Lake: Centennial History Book Committee, 1984).

4. 1930 Census of Population figures. On the Yankee stream of migration to the upper Midwest, see John C. Hudson, "Yankeeland in the Middle West," *Journal of Geography* 85 (September-October, 1986), 195-200.

5. On the process of settlement into the area, see Robert C. Ostergren, "Geographic Perspectives on the History of Settlement in the Upper Midwest," *Upper Midwest History* 1(1981), 27-39; Ostergren, "European Settlement and Ethnicity Patterns on the Agricultural Frontiers of South Dakota," *South Dakota History* 13 (Spring-Summer, 1983), 49-82; John C. Hudson, "Two Dakota Homestead Frontiers," *Annals of the Association of American Geographers* 63 (December, 1973), 442-62; Hudson, "Migration to an American Frontier," Ibid. 66 (June, 1976), 242-65.

6. An article in the *Clear Lake Courier-Advocate* (June 20, 1941) took off from a recent story in the *Minneapolis Star Journal*, which awarded the title of "champion church city of the country" to Fergus Falls, Minnesota, which had nineteen churches in a population of 10,848, giving it a ratio of one church for every 571 residents. Other towns contested the claim, Canby, for instance, noting that it had nine churches and a population of 2,099, a ratio of 1:233. The *Courier-Advocate* editor, joining in the spirit of the thing, argued that with eight churches in a population of 995, and a ratio of 1:124, Clear Lake had a logical claim to be the champion church city of the world.

7. In 1940, under the auspices of the Ministerial Association, approximately 900 persons in 258 family units were surveyed (of a total population in the town of 997). Of the total who were polled, 315 attended church regularly, 162 went to church occasionally, and the rest never went. Of the 460 parents reporting, 192 were regular church attenders, 94 went occasionally, and 174 never attended. *Clear Lake Courier-Advocate*, March 1, 1940.

8. The local newspaper published reports on enrollment trends calculated by South Dakota State College Extension Sociologist W. F. Kumlien. *Clear Lake Courier-Advocate*, May 30, June 13, 20, 1941.

9. The eight town schools were Altamont, Astoria, Brandt, Clear Lake, Gary, Goodwin, School for the Blind (Gary), and Toronto. *Deuel County Advocate*, April 19, 1934.

10. *Clear Lake Courier-Advocate*, September 13, 1940.

11. *Deuel County Advocate*, July 23, 1936.

12. *Deuel County Advocate*, May 11, 1933.

13. *Clear Lake Courier-Advocate*, July 4, 1941.

14. *Deuel County Advocate*, November 16, 23, 1933.

15. On Armistice Day, too, most businesses, except garages, filling stations, and some places selling food, closed for the day.

16. *Deuel County Advocate*, July 2, 1936.

17. *Clear Lake Courier-Advocate*, June 6, 1941.

18. *Deuel County Advocate*, October 28, November 4, 11, 1937, October 13, 27, 1939, October 25, 1940.

19. *Clear Lake Courier-Advocate*, May 10, 1940. That Clear Lake residents were not entirely unfamiliar with the game is indicated by a paragraph item in the paper two years earlier noting a local American Legion and Home Guard team going to Castlewood for a game. Deuel County Advocate, December 8, 1938.

20. *Clear Lake Courier-Advocate*, October 29, 1942, April 19, 1945.

21. *Deuel County Advocate*, March 5, October 1, 1931.

22. *Clear Lake Courier-Advocate*, February 17, 1944.

23. *Clear Lake Courier-Advocate*, July 4, 1941.

24. For example, see the quarter-page ad in the *Deuel County Advocate* (October 4, 1934) titled "Let's Be Fair to Our Home Town Merchants."

25. *Deuel County Advocate*, June 28, 1930.

26. *Deuel County Advocate*, October 11, 1934.

27. *Deuel County Advocate*, October 15, 1931.

28. *Clear Lake Courier-Advocate*, February 12, 1942.

Discussion Questions:

1. Can you remember what life was like in small towns during the 1930s and 1940s, or have you heard stories about it?

2. How was life in Clear Lake (and in your own community) during the 30s and 40s different from what it is today, and how was it similar?

3. What difference did it make that there was relatively little racial and ethnic diversity in Clear Lake during the 30s and 40s?

4. What difference did people's gender make in their status and power in the community during the 30s and 40s? Are things better or worse now in this regard?

5. What impact did World War II have on community in Clear Lake? Compare this with the impacts that the Korean War, Vietnam War, the Gulf War, and the War in Iraq have had on community in the United States.

The Kidd Kids

Darla Bielfeldt

When the Kidd family lived on the south side of town
In a metal quonset, half-barreled, and noisy in the rain,
I envied them the curved roof above their heads.
It rose so surely to enter or yield to the sky. But outside,
Gallon-sized cans from their aunt's restaurant littered the yard,
Lying where their dog had rolled them with his tongue seeking
Scraps still stuck to the rusty metal.
Inside, I imagined the Kidd kids lying in their beds at night,
Their calming roofline shielding them, softening edges.

But the daughter Hannah yielded young to the strangers of summer,
Bore a son when I was ten years old. She rolled out of town
Pulling a pop-up camper, following blocks and blocks of combines.
Her brother John's arm was soft beneath the blade of his knife
As he drew hearts and blood before the morning recess. When we
    were sixteen
He was smothered inside a metal grain bin, standing
On the cement floor when the new grain rushed in, hailing him.
He could never reach the top, and when they found him
He was pressed against the curved side, his open mouth full of wheat.

And last summer I saw the youngest, Bloyd, working at a county fair,
A tattooed carney just passing through again, rank and soft and slow,
Blowing shaky haloes over children's heads as they lined up, waiting
To enter his inflated and portable castle.

Discussion Questions:

1. There are images of human dwellings throughout the poem. What do those images suggest?

2. The poem describes a community set in a place and two communities in motion. What might some of the differences be?

3. Minneapolis and St. Paul are usually referred to as "the Twin Cities." To what extent might that term apply to all communities? What are the twin cities in the poem? What are the twin cities where you live?

Rebuilding the Circle:
Tribal Philosophies of Community

Elden Lawrence

Communities are groups of people who live together in one place and share some things in common. If the sharing allows for self-expression and human interactions, the community can be strong. A strong community is one that immerses itself in the infallible wisdom and truth of the Golden Rule. Traditional tribal society provides one of the purest examples of authentic community life, because traditional tribal community extends beyond common interest endeavors and civic responsibilities. However, this generation of keepers of the community spirit may be the last one, unless lessons are learned. These lessons must be learned. If they are, traditional American Indian society could contribute significantly to the preservation and deepening of traditional community for all peoples.

The traditional American Indian society lived in an ecosystem governed by natural laws. Living in close harmony with creation, traditional tribal people cultivated unique relationships with all living things, regarding the earth as the mother of all things. George Catlin, the American artist who traveled and painted his way through the west in the 1830's, painted some authentic pictures, both on canvas and in the minds of people:

I love a people who have always made me welcome to the best they had . . . who are honest without laws, who have no jails and no poor houses . . . who never take the name of God in vain . . . who worship

God without a Bible, and I believe God loves them also . . . who are free from religious animosities . . . who have never raised a hand against me, or stolen my property, where there is no law to punish either . . . who never fought a battle with white men except on their own ground . . . and Oh, how I love a people who don't live for the love of money![1]

What Catlin was experiencing was true traditional tribalism. It had been honed and shaped by centuries of trial and adjustments. Indian people tried to reduce matters to their simplest forms. In the Scriptures, the Lord says all laws of humanity and relationships can be fulfilled by obeying just two; love God with all your heart, soul, strength and mind and love your neighbor as yourself. Centuries of living in close contact in small village environments necessitated the adoption of an accommodating lifestyle that embodied Christian ideals.

Christian missionaries did not have to teach the Indians to love their neighbors. In fact, the sharing habits of the Indians caused the missionaries much concern. They thought that what they thought of as hardships of life should be incentive for traditional Indians to want to adopt the so-called "civilized" lifestyle of the Americans. But the Indian people found it too difficult to enjoy personal comforts when their relatives were suffering from want, regardless of the reason. The American government and the Christian missionaries also believed that the Indians should become individualized and competitive. Christian missionary Stephen R. Riggs emphatically stated the argument that Indians had to change their lifestyle or be eliminated:

It is well understood by all thinking persons, that in their present uncivilized condition, they cannot long continue. Civilization, as it passes onward, must encircle them with its blessings, or sweep them from the face of the earth. They must be civilized and Christianized or perish.[2]

So the federal government initiated assimilation policies to end tribalism and individualize Indian people. Conventional wisdom of the time was that placing Indians on individual tracts of land would inspire the competitive selfishness that was at the base of civilization. Having all things in common and not desiring a better home than one's neighbor was a hindrance to "progress." The Dawes Act of 1887, the Allotment Act, ended tribal ownership of land and assigned tracts of land to individuals. The agent for the Yankton Sioux wrote in 1877:

> As long as Indians live in villages they will retain many of their old and injurious habits. Frequent feasts, community in food, heathen ceremonies, and dances, constant visiting—these will continue as long as the people live together in close neighborhoods and villages ... I trust that before another year is ended they will generally be located upon individual lands of farms. From that date will begin their real and permanent progress.[3]

In the early Dakota society, all things were held in common and everyone shared equally in work, hunting and the harvesting of game. There was an absence of selfishness and greed because what was believed to be moral conduct was a high priority. A traditional Indian's identity came from his family and his village. If he did wrong, he disgraced his family and his village. He honored them if he did well. He lived in an extended family. His aunts and uncles were second parents. His cousins were like brothers and sisters. Young children grew up with many teachers, mentors and role models.

In contrast, the spirit of capitalism is strongest in the United States. Private ownership of the means of production and distribution defines this economic system that dominates other socioeconomic systems. However, when what he possesses, regardless of how he obtains it, determines the worth of a person, then there is corruption and violations of human rights. Influence is a capital that can be economized and conversely, money can buy influence for sordid gains. Capitalists understand that allegiance to money has to have the highest priority. Love of money then overshadows moral laws. A successful capitalist must not only control his own means of wealth, production and distribution; he must also control other people's capitalistic ventures as well.

Eventually, a number of federal laws and regulations dismantled tribalism and traditional communal living, even though Indian groups are still called "tribes." However, strands of the old system continue to exist and remnants of the old cultural communal practices are still recognized. I was fortunate to be born at a time when some of these communal practices were still in existence. What replaced the old system were events and practices that derived from the Indian Christian churches. There was some compatibility between some of the church doings and the old community society of the Dakotas, as well as some differences.

The churches, in the absence of traditional tribal government, performed most of the social functions in those early days of my childhood. Church elders made regular visits to the homes and neighbors paid frequent visits. There were regular social gatherings at different homes for visits and games. Homes were full of people, and even though food was very scarce, it seemed there was plenty to share. Whist card parties went into the early morning hours and sometimes the host home would make a place on the floor for the younger children to lie down and sleep. Families would travel with horses, wagons, and sometime horse-drawn sleds. Houses heated with wood-burning stoves meant getting home to a cold house. However, no one seemed to choose to stay home unless sick. There was great satisfaction in this type of personal interaction that you cannot get from sitting and watching television. The best card players and storytellers among them were well known. Everyone seemed to have needs and everyone seemed willing to share what they had. This is what may have kept the sacred hoop from totally fading away.

Even though there were no telephones to make inquiries, parents didn't get overly concerned when their children were at their neighbors and didn't come home at night. Children often stayed over with their neighbor friends, and while they were there, they became a part of those families, doing chores or taking part in family activities. One elderly woman, now deceased, once said to me, "I'm proud of what you have done with yourself—I was your second mother." It made me feel good that others shared in what I may have accomplished. I believe that is what true community is all about.

I recently talked with a tribal elder about the breakdown of family values and the dysfunction of contemporary tribal society, and he said that until forty years ago, we had a low suicide rate, but now we are leaders in that category. He talked about how we are losing our coping power and how our children now prefer the dominant society's norms and trends. He said the children now prefer to sit at the foot of a TV instead of at the feet of their elders.

I asked him if we could prevent further decline of our culture. He said the best we could do was to retain what we had left, and that only if we worked hard at it. "When culture is devalued," he explained, "it loses its respect and dies. It's like having a heart attack. Part of the heart dies, and that part can never live again. Some people try to substitute something in its place, but it's not the same. I believe it's better to leave it alone." He went on to say: "When a dog gets old and he knows he's going to die soon, he wanders off somewhere where no one can find him and he dies. He leaves with you his memory, but he will not return." I think what he meant was that culture can never be completely revitalized. It never comes back the same and therefore is best left alone.

I then asked another tribal elder about these matters. He told me that he had also seen many changes over the years. He said: "At one time we were together as a people. We helped each other with what little we had. We had small farms and everyone went to church on Sundays. Some people walked as far as ten miles to church. We had respect for each other and ourselves. Our leaders went to see you to find out what you needed. There wasn't any money to give, but people would help in other ways. With the small farms, gardens and a little wild game, we were able to get by. It wasn't much, but we did it ourselves. We lived simple and didn't need much. No one seemed to be ashamed to be poor."

He went on to say that the fall of the stock market in the late twenties did not greatly affect the lifestyle of the Indians because they were already unemployed and not dependent on trade markets, nor did the wars during the first half of the 20th century. What did devastate the people, he said, was the Great Depression, when the Indians lost their farms and were without means to support themselves. Then there was much sickness, including epidemics of whooping cough and diphtheria in 1939. Because their faith was weak, or as he put it, "their hearts were weak," they lost their balance. Alcohol soon became a way to numb their pain and miseries and enable them to live in a different world. He said, "The evil one found a way to deceive the poor Indian and it's been that way since."

Experiencing hardship was nothing new to traditional tribal people. Contrary to Longfellow's stereotypical, nostalgic impression of native culture, the traditional hunting and gathering culture was a hard way of life. The native people strived to live with nature and never sought the home comforts Europeans thought necessary. Samuel Pond wrote this about the old culture in his book *The Dakota or Sioux in Minnesota As They Were in 1834*:

> It is a prevalent opinion that Indians in a savage state spend most of their time in idleness, and those who have known the Dakotas only since they have received annuities for their land may suppose that they never made much exertion to obtain a livelihood; but if they had accompanied them through one year in 1834, they would have learned that they did not contrive to live without hard labor, also that they did not shrink from hard work, but acted like men who were determined to take care of themselves and their families. If they had been as indolent and inefficient as many think they were, we should never have heard of them, for they all would have perished long ago.[4]

However, the hardships resulting from capitalistic pressures were overpoweringly destructive. The eventual distribution of government food surplus lacked the personal compassionate sharing of the traditional tribal community. I lived through a time when there was no welfare or government food stamps or commodities and I witnessed some of the changes to tribal society when food surplus was first distributed. Early on, there was some hoarding and unequal distributions, but for the most part, no one made much complaint. But the extended family concept had diminished and now the immediate family received the attention. The

Indian people came to expect that immediate family members and close relatives would be the first ones to receive care. That is why support from large families now greatly determines tribal election outcomes.

Now tribal community consists of four groups: those who work for the tribe and maintain close contact with the tribal council and tribal programs; those who work for the United States Government (BIA or Indian Health Service); those who live in and out of tribal and non-tribal societies; and the last of the true traditional people, who will be gone in another five to ten years. The last two groups are ones who have kept tribal communal traditions alive and managed to better interact with the non-Indians.

The true traditional people are mostly the elderly who have remained on the outside of mainstream white and contemporary Indian societies. They maintain simple social habits and do not involve themselves with complicated socioeconomic situations. They are the pillars of traditional tribal society. They are the ones who most non-Indians think all Indians are. But although they possess many of the old cultural values and principles, they are largely ignored by both non-traditional Indians and non-Indians.

The ones who work for the tribe think and operate like the self-help programs with which they are associated. It's enough that they come to work and are there for eight hours. A lot of them are political appointees and this practice undermines the program manager's ability to increase the employee's productivity. Employee turnover and job switching are common. Tribal employees are similar to union workers. Political leaders know they need the support of the tribal employees to get elected. Tribal employees will go to the polls and vote while many others refuse, or neglect to vote. Indian politicians know they can win an election primarily with the tribal employee vote.

The BIA and Indian Health are institutions a person can retire to while still "working." Once you're in, you can stay as long as you choose. The pay and benefits are good and you don't have to be productive. In fact, if you try to work too hard you might have problems. BIA and IHS employees are encouraged to stay out of tribal politics and tribal affairs.

As a result, they usually stay out of community affairs. The BIA is bureaucratically situated and can maintain control of tribal affairs and yet be out of the direct line of fire of any dissident actions.

Most of the people in the tribe are out of the loop and have contact with the tribe primarily through the programs in which they participate. They are people of limited means and depend on the services the tribe provides. Government programs are now attempting to do some of the things once done through compassion in the old culture. Some physical needs get attention, but the community spirit is not improved. Instead, the tribal leaders get recognition or criticism for the service distribution.

So, the principle of reciprocal giving is lacking. Only the older tribal members who remember the hard times of the past seem to show any real gratitude for what they receive. The Tribal Elderly Program provides nutritious meals at a reduced cost and delivers meals to those unable to get to the elderly center. The tribe also provides each tribal elder with $100 every four months. This distribution takes place at the tribe's casino. Unfortunately, a lot of the money goes right back into the slot machines and never leaves the building. The federal government, according to its specifications, provides the majority of the funds for tribal programs.

However, versions of the old communal practices continue and still provide the foundation for tribal community life. One of the most significant of these practices is the charity benefit given for someone who has lost his or her house or other possessions. The person's social standing doesn't seem to matter; people turn out and give what they can. Most of the participants give out of their essentials and not out of their excess. If a benefit auction is held, the people will bid way beyond the material value of the object. Friends and relatives of the hardship victim will also purchase small items and make up baskets to auction. At the other extreme, valuable star quilts and other items of personal value will be donated and often bring in less than their value. I have participated in benefits for Indians and also for non-Indians; and despite their smaller wealth and numbers, Indians give more.

Another practice that is a version from the old culture is the giveaway or honoring ceremony. When a loved one passes away, there is usually a period of mourning followed by a traditional giveaway. Usually those persons selected as pallbearers receive beautiful star quilts and significant others will receive other gifts. Every person who attends these ceremonies receives some item. Some of these items are held dear by the recipients and are kept as memorials. Communal practices such as the giveaway and the honoring ceremonies are open to anyone, including non-Indians. On occasion, the Indian people honor non-Indians. Traditional drum groups will provide an honor song and the honored person will receive a traditional star quilt. This is one of the greatest honors the Indians bestow on any person.

The "wopida" ceremony is a practice that originally was a joyous celebration. It is also a time for gathering to bring the people back together after some incident or situation has caused a separation of the people. Recently, the veterans of my tribe staged a takeover of the tribal headquarters and families of opposing sides were in a sensitive situation. One of the elder members of the tribe organized a wopida and all the people of the opposing sides were encouraged to attend. A traditional meal was provided at the expense of the organizer and some supporters. In the old days, traditional enemies were given a feast to end a potential battle between the two groups. I believe this ceremony actualizes the concept of asking and giving forgiveness and everyone leaving the wopida feels better.

In the final analysis, the federal government has created a permanent welfare state on Indian reservations that is alive and well. Government programs are a way of life, as is the tribal political system. Crime and suicide statistics are on the rise and most of the criminal acts are committed against tribal members. The sacred hoop exists only in the minds of some people. Modern traditional practices will not mend the broken hoop but it's a good idea to try. Finally, having said all this, I could be wrong, but I could just as well be right.

Hau!

Elden, He Mi-ye Do! (That's Who I Am)

97

Notes:

1. Armstrong, Virginia Irving. *I Have Spoken*. Chicago: The Swallow Press, 1971, p. 70.

2. Riggs, Stephen R. *The Dakota Language*. St. Paul: Minnesota Historical Collections, MHS, 1850, p. 89.

3. Cohen, Felix S. *Handbook of Federal Indian Law*. Washington: U.S. Government Printing Office, 1941, p. 208.

4. Pond, Samuel W. *The Dakota or Sioux As They Were in 1834*. St. Paul: Minnesota Historical Society Press, 1986, p. 43.

Discussion Questions:

1. Is the past past? Can "old ways" be restored? Why or why not?

2. Is it possible to reconcile the contrasting ideas of "community" found in this essay? If not, why not? If so, how might that reconciliation be achieved?

Turning the Notion of "Community" on Its Head: SDSU-Flandreau Indian School Success Academy

MaryJo Benton Lee

For a critical sociologist, particularly one from South Dakota, writing about "community" is problematic. Here "community" has often been understood in terms of the exclusion of those who are different—specifically, people of color and the underclasses.

Sociology provides valuable thinking tools for understanding social interaction—and the lack of it. But simple understanding is not enough. We should also be committed to social justice and institutional change and use our sociological understanding to improve the human condition.

Sometimes life gives us the opportunity to do just that. Such an opportunity appeared for me, and for my university, in the fall of 2000. Teachers and staff members from the Flandreau Indian School asked South Dakota State University to partner with them in a college preparatory program for Native American students. As a result, South Dakota State University-Flandreau Indian School Success Academy was born, and nothing has been quite the same at either school ever since.

Background

South Dakota State University, where I work as a sociologist, is a predominantly white, land-grant institution located in the middle of Indian Country. Nearly ten percent of our state's population is American Indian. About one percent of our university's student body—and far less than one percent of its faculty and staff—is American Indian. This is troubling for a land-grant university with the express mission of serving all of the people of the state.

Add to this the fact that American Indian people living on South Dakota's nine reservations experience some of the nation's highest rates of poverty, unemployment and fetal alcohol syndrome. These problems cry out for solutions by people, Native and non-Native, trained in fields like engineering, agriculture, pharmacy, nursing, education, and family and consumer sciences, fields that form the academic backbone of South Dakota State University.

History

South Dakota State University was founded in 1881. Ten years earlier, just 20 miles away, a Presbyterian mission school was founded to educate Indian children living near the big bend of the Sioux River. That school became the Flandreau Indian School. Today FIS is the oldest continually-operating federal Indian boarding school in the country. FIS enrolls up to 375 students per year. These students, who are in grades nine through twelve, come from about 20 states and 50 tribes.

Contact between South Dakota State University and the Flandreau Indian School was limited to non-existent for most of their histories, until the fall of 2000. At that time, FIS was experiencing increasing problems. Dropout rates were high, and academic performance was low. Most students who began school at FIS as freshmen did not complete high school there as seniors. Among the few who did, only a handful continued on to higher education.

Consequently, FIS teachers and administrators decided to undertake a major school reform effort, under the direction of an energetic new superintendent. They approached South Dakota State University for help. I was fortunate to be the initial point of contact between FIS and SDSU. As diversity coordinator for SDSU's College of Engineering, I had previously arranged for FIS students to attend our annual Engineering Exploration Days, so I was a "familiar face."

The question put forth by the teachers and administrators from FIS was simple: Would SDSU partner with FIS in a program that would expose students to college and to the careers open to college graduates? It was hoped that such exposure to the long-term possibilities of post-secondary education would create incentives for students to stay in school and to achieve academically in the short term. SDSU's University Diversity Council, led by its diversity enhancement director, said "yes" and supplied the initial funding.

The president of South Dakota State University, Peggy Gordon Miller, and the superintendent of the Flandreau Indian School, Betty Belkham, signed a memorandum of understanding, committing their institutions to narrowing the educational achievement gap between Indian and non-Indian students. This provided the foundation for the new partnership.

The school reform efforts underway at FIS at the time were guided by a Talent Development High School Model, developed at Johns Hopkins University. The freshman year activities in the TDHS Model were called "Success Academy," so the fledgling SDSU-FIS program took its name from that effort.

SDSU-FIS Success Academy began as a one-semester program for FIS freshmen, run out of the SDSU College of Engineering. Each year saw the addition of another cohort to the program (sophomores, juniors and then seniors). Today Success Academy is a comprehensive four-year college preparatory program involving all freshmen and sophomores and all college-bound juniors and seniors attending the Flandreau Indian School. More than 250 faculty and staff members from all eight of SDSU's academic colleges and from the Student Affairs Division have served as presenters and planners for Success Academy programming.

Success Academy is a grassroots effort, made possible, in large part, by in-kind contributions of faculty time and financial support by SDSU's deans. More recently, funding has also been provided by the vice president for Academic Affairs. The SDSU College of Engineering remains Success Academy's home on campus, supplying clerical support, office space and the coordinator.

I coordinate Success Academy for South Dakota State University. Sandra Koester, my counterpart at the Flandreau Indian School, serves as

Success Academy principal. Our efforts are directed by a steering committee composed of administrators, faculty, staff and students, from FIS and SDSU, Indian and non-Indian.

"Let us put our minds together and see what kind of future we can build for our children," said the great Hunkpapa Lakota chief Sitting Bull in 1876. These words guide our work.

Success Academy and Communities of Difference

For most people, "community" is real and concrete. Norms are shared by the members of a given community, and this kind of consensus is assumed to be generally positive. But what would happen if we turned the traditional notion of "community" on its head? What if we were to posit that consensus may not be reached, and that, in fact, consensus should not be reached? Critical theorist William G. Tierney (1993:23-26) does just this in his book, *Building Communities of Difference: Higher Education in the Twenty-First Century*.

Using the principles of Martin Luther King, Jr., Tierney suggests that postsecondary institutions become communities of brotherly love and service to humanity, based on the principle of agape or "selfless love" (Tierney 1993:23). King (1958:105) defined agape this way: "It is love in action. Agape is love seeking to preserve and create community. It is insistence on community even when one seeks to break it. Agape is a willingness to sacrifice in the interest of mutuality. Agape is a willingness to go to any length to restore community." Tierney says that, in higher education, this means accepting one another's differences and working from those differences to build solidarity. Tierney (1993:140) argues that for too long "male, heterosexual, Eurocentric" voices in the academy have been privileged, while other voices have been silenced. Tierney (1993:25) says we now need to "develop the notion of difference and engage in dialogues across border zones." In other words, Tierney recommends that we build the idea of community around the concept of diversity.

We could look at the Flandreau Indian School and South Dakota State University, at the most simple level, as two separate communities—one predominantly Native, the other predominantly white; one focused on K-12 education, the other engaged in higher education; and so forth. But Tierney argues, as I will, that a multiplicity of cultures exists within schools as well as between schools. We must start by accepting cultural differences—between Indians and non-Indians, between people with recognized educational credentials and people with other forms of knowledge, between the young and the old, to name just a few. We can then use this acceptance of difference to build solidarity. Only in this way can we hope to achieve our goals.

The South Dakota State University-Flandreau Indian School Success Academy has two goals. The first goal is help more American Indian students prepare for and succeed in college. The second goal is to make South Dakota State University into the kind of place where that can happen. Both are equally important.

Mutuality of need by two academic communities, FIS and SDSU, provides the scaffolding upon which the Success Academy program rests. Betty Belkham, the chief school administrator at the Flandreau Indian School, has said that FIS students, because they go to an all-American Indian high school, would not be truly prepared to enter the diverse world that awaits them after graduation without a program like Success Academy. The same holds true for South Dakota State University students, who attend an overwhelmingly white university, an environment far different from the ones in which most of them will work as college graduates.

In SDSU-FIS Success Academy, we build communities of difference to achieve our common goals and to meet our mutual needs. We build communities of difference three ways—by prolonged involvement, by honoring identities and by reinventing cultural capital. The following three sections will further explain those three ways of building communities of difference.

Building Communities across Difference by Prolonged Involvement

On our website, we describe SDSU-FIS Success Academy as "an early and intensive college preparatory program for Native American high school students." These two adjectives are what set this program apart from others, and they are what unite the academic communities of South Dakota State University and the Flandreau Indian School in this endeavor.

Early. Success Academy first engages FIS students in the college preparatory process when they are freshmen in high school. Recent research has shown that early adolescence is when most students make critical decisions about their life chances and when they decide whether post-secondary education is possible. Thus, most college preparatory programs, which focus their attention on high school juniors and seniors, miss the mark.

SDSU-FIS Success Academy involves all of the freshmen and sophomores who attend the Flandreau Indian School. Thus, Success Academy "assumes success" (Tierney 2000:225). The message is clear: Every FIS student is expected to complete high school and to consider post-secondary education of some kind—technical college, community college, tribal college, four-year college or university. Success Academy provides numerous structures to ensure that students do just that. While the program acknowledges that barriers exist, it simultaneously teaches students strategies to overcome them (Tierney 2000:228).

Intensive. All 100 freshmen come to SDSU for seven full-day visits during their first year at the Flandreau Indian School. Students rotate through hands-on workshops in all seven of SDSU's academic colleges: Engineering, Pharmacy, Nursing, Arts and Science, Education and Counseling, Family and Consumer Sciences, and Agriculture and Biological Sciences.

All 100 FIS sophomores come to SDSU for four full-day visits during their second year in high school. These visits focus on four areas identified by the first cohort of Success Academy students as being of particular interest to them and not covered in the freshman year program. The sophomore visits include a Focus on the Arts Day, a Focus on the Military Day, a Focus on American Indian Studies Day and a Focus on Health, Physical Education and Recreation Day.

Freshmen and sophomores are accompanied on their Success Academy visits to SDSU by teachers and aides from the Flandreau Indian

School. By the end of an FIS student's sophomore year, he or she has spent 11 full days on a college campus. Each visit to the SDSU campus is an opportunity for FIS students to picture themselves successfully attending classes and events as college students.

The frequency of campus visits, the length of the visits and the number of students served all require a tremendous investment of time and effort by faculty and staff at South Dakota State University. Since the fall of 2000, more than 250 faculty and staff have presented Success Academy workshops, served on planning committees and otherwise assisted with programming. Most faculty and staff members have involved SDSU students as co-presenters and planners.

"Success Academy is the premier diversity program at SDSU because it directly engages faculty members and students with American Indian people," says Allen Branum, the university's Director for Diversity Enhancement. "No amount of classroom diversity training can compare with personally getting to know American Indian individuals and learning from them their hopes, dreams, issues and rich cultural heritage."

Tierney (1993:142), writing from a critical theory perspective, says that "prolonged involvement" is the only way that communities of difference can transcend the borders separating them and work together to empower students:

We come to understand one another not by broad, sweeping actions, but by living and learning on a daily basis. We are not tourists on a week-long excursion with a guidebook in our hands to show us the interesting sites and lives of a people. To the contrary, we cannot understand differences in a momentary fragmentary fashion, and we do not have a Michelin guide to tell us what to do. Instead, we engage people where we are most at risk with questioning our own identities, and we do so through prolonged involvement . . . By "prolonged involvement," I mean that learning about the Other never stops; we are always in a process of redefinition.

Building Communities across Difference by Honoring Identities

Prolonged involvement is one characteristic that sets SDSU-FIS Success Academy apart from other college preparatory programs serving students of color. Honoring identities is another characteristic that makes Success Academy unique.

Many other college preparatory programs treat students of color as if they are "broken and in need of repair" (Tierney 2000:223) in order to fit into the existing, predominantly white, academic community. Success Academy takes a different approach, one centered around the idea of "community cultural wealth" (Yosso 2005).

In Success Academy, we de-emphasize the notion that students need, first and foremost, cultural capital to succeed in school. Pierre Bourdieu (1977, 1986) defines "cultural capital" as a collection of knowledge, skills and abilities possessed and inherited by privileged groups in society. Bourdieu says cultural capital is acquired from one's family and through formal schooling. Some examples of cultural capital include having formally educated parents who can help with studying, living in an area with good schools, possessing adequate communication skills in the mainstream language and having access to reading materials and computers. The key point is that dominant groups maintain their power by limiting access to cultural capital itself and by limiting opportunities for learning how to use this capital to achieve upward social mobility (Yosso 2005:76).

By contrast, SDSU-FIS Success Academy is built on the foundation of community cultural wealth, as it has been explained by critical race theorist Tara J. Yosso (2005). Success Academy is based on respect for the families, communities and tribes from which our students come. In Success Academy, we acknowledge that our students, who in more traditional programs might be labeled "at risk," in fact bring to school with them a tremendous reserve of assets derived from lives lived as American Indians resisting oppression.

Here are some ways that we honor our students' identities and recognize the community cultural wealth they bring to South Dakota State University through their involvement in Success Academy:

• Freshman workshops range from "Wokunze — A Life Pathway in Nursing" to "Native Americans and Journalism — 21st Century Storytellers," both led by Native American professors. Sophomore Focus on the Military Day, led by the Aerospace Studies and Military Science Departments, centers around the theme of "Native Americans in the Military: Past, Present and Future." That day includes a film on American Indian military heroes and a talk by a cadet who is an enrolled member of the Sisseton-Wahpeton Sioux Tribe. It is important for our students to see their cultures reflected in the SDSU curriculum and in those who teach.

• Success Academy workshops expose students not only to college, but also to the careers open to college graduates. The program emphasizes career areas identified by tribal leaders as being of critical need in their communities, for example, engineering, agriculture, education, pharmacy, nursing, journalism and nutrition. It is important for our students to see the ways that college can help them "come full circle" (Garrod and Larimore 1997:15), that is, ways they can apply knowledge to serve their people.

• Following afternoon Success Academy workshops, freshmen and sophomores stay on campus for evening meals, attended by the afternoon workshop presenters and hosted by the SDSU Native American Club. The club includes a number of Success Academy scholars who have graduated from FIS and who are now attending SDSU. It is important for our young FIS students to interact with strong positive role models of successful Native college students.

• After their dinners on campus, freshmen and sophomore Success Academy scholars stay on campus and attend university events. These events have included a performance by hoop dancer Jackie Bird and an exhibition by noted Indian painter Arthur Amiotte. It is important for our students to see their arts and traditions celebrated by the larger campus community.

• Many evening events directly address issues of prejudice and discrimination, in education and in the larger society. Geraldine Goes In Center tells the story of the Wounded Knee Massacre from the Native perspective. Jerome Kills Small portrays Dr. Charles Eastman, a 19th century Dakota physician who grappled throughout his lifetime with issues of biculturalism. It is important for our students to see—and to learn from—Native people who engage in "oppositional behavior that challenges inequality" (Yosso 2005:80).

• Each academic year ends with a commencement ceremony, recognizing all the Success Academy scholars who have participated in the program during the previous nine months. Scholars walk across the stage and receive plaques, engraved with their names, from SDSU's vice president and deans. Success Academy ceremonies typically include an honor song, acknowledging the scholars' commitment to furthering their educations. The commencement speech is delivered by a prominent Native American leader, such as State Senator Ron Volesky in 2001 and Miss South Dakota, Vanessa Shortbull, in 2004. It is important for our students to hear firsthand from Native people about "maintaining hopes and dreams for the future, even in the face of real and perceived barriers" (Yosso 2005:77).

At the end of Success Academy's first year, we asked our students to work together to create a logo and a motto for the new program. Their final design was a medicine wheel with the words underneath reading "Success Academy—Where All Students Are Honored Students." Without overt explanation by us as teachers, our students identified the cultural scaffolding that supports the entire Success Academy endeavor.

Building Communities across Difference by Reinventing Cultural Capital

Cultural capital, a term conceived by Bourdieu (1977, 1986), was narrowly defined as a resource inherited by sons and daughters of the elite and passed on via the system of formal schooling. Society was seen as divided between the educational "haves" and the educational "have nots." Those fortunate enough to have been born into power and privilege used those resources to sustain their positions, to the detriment of those less fortunate. This fundamentally pessimistic and fatalistic view of cultural reproduction held sway for about a quarter century.

While most critical theorists would agree that academic success is still largely dictated by the extent to which an individual absorbs the dominant culture, the concept of cultural capital has been reinvented. Cultural capital is now understood much more broadly to be a set of skills that can be taught by "a state-sponsored source" (Mehan et al. 1996:216). SDSU-FIS Success Academy is just such a source. Success Academy aspires to be "an instrument . . . of social equity" (Mehan et al. 1996:217-218), striving to pass on cultural capital to the students it serves. Here are some examples of how junior and senior year students "learn the skills, manners, norms presumably inherited by elite students" (Mehan et al. 1996:217) through the Success Academy program:

• The first two years of Success Academy, which involve all of the freshmen and sophomores at FIS, create an interest in and an excitement about college. The last two years of Success Academy involve only those juniors and seniors who plan to continue on to post-secondary education. In junior and senior year Success Academy, we work with our students to turn college dreams into realities. About 25 FIS juniors come to South Dakota State University for four half-day sessions in March and April. By the time they have completed their junior year of high school, Success Academy scholars have spent 15 days on the campus of SDSU. Frequent visits to a college campus—and the feeling of belonging that comes with those visits—is an example of the kind of cultural capital generated within the Success Academy program. Children of upper-class origin, who live at home with their immediate families, routinely visit college campuses and explore post-secondary opportunities, and this increases the likelihood that they will attend college after high school. Success Academy makes such opportunities available to FIS students, whose relatives live too far away to facilitate such college visits.

• Junior year session topics range from "Making the Decision to Attend College" and "Paying for a College Education" to "Choosing Your

Major" and "So What's Next." These topics are regularly discussed with the sons and daughters of the elite, but Success Academy scholars are disadvantaged in this regard. In most cases, they will be first generation college students, and while attending FIS they are geographically separated from their relatives. So engaging our Success Academy students in the discussion of such topics contributes, at least in small part, to leveling the playing field.

• SDSU's Student Affairs Division bears most of the responsibility for the junior year Success Academy program. This is significant because it gives Success Academy scholars a chance to make essential connections with key staff members in offices like Admissions, Financial Aid and Native American Student Advisement (just as more traditional high school students, who visit campus with their parents, do).

• The Success Academy program matches up each of the juniors with an "academic parent." "Academic parents" are retired (and some current) SDSU faculty members who work one-on-one with the juniors. The "academic parents" have lunch with the Success Academy juniors, discuss with them their plans for higher education and accompany them on campus visits to the academic departments in which the students intend to major. Many "academic parents" and their students keep in touch with each other long after the junior year program ends. "Academic parents" provide cultural capital in the form of instrumental and emotional support for American Indian students navigating through a university system not created with Native people in mind. While the retired faculty members at other universities are often a marginalized and under-utilized community of scholars, in Success Academy, retired faculty members are treasured as priceless resources, benefiting our students and our institution. This is in keeping with our Native students' respect for elders.

• Each fall 10 Success Academy seniors have the opportunity of signing up for a special section of SDSU's Basic Writing course. These seniors are enrolled as concurrent high school/SDSU students. The class meets twice a week, once in the Lakota-Dakota conference room at SDSU and once in a classroom at FIS. The Success Academy scholars earn three college credits when they complete the course. Another course, Basic Algebra, is offered to the same cohort of students during the spring semester. Thus the Success Academy seniors earn six college credits before they finish high school and are better prepared to undertake college-level English and mathematics courses. In the Success Academy classroom, if not in the family, seniors learn such things as the values of timeliness, orderliness, and neatness; methods of challenging questionable policies or decisions; and how to talk to professors in college. These are all examples of cultural capital accrued (Mehan et al. 1996:216).

• On certain nights throughout the academic year, the FIS seniors stay at SDSU after class for dinner and hands-on work sessions. During the work sessions, students complete college applications, apply for financial aid, prepare for the ACT test and again visit the academic departments in which they intend to major. All of these activities constitute cultural capital and would be the norm in homes where children live year-around and where parents are college-educated. The senior year program is made possible by generous contributions from several diverse communities willing to invest in American Indian education—the Citigroup Foundation (through Citibank South Dakota), the National Aeronautics and Space Administration (through the South Dakota Space Grant Consortium), and the South Dakota Association of Christian Churches (through the Flandreau Indian Chaplaincy, which provides the seniors' transportation to and from the SDSU campus). This investment, year after year, results in as many as 10 Success Academy scholars being admitted to college by the time they graduate from high school.

In discussing cultural capital (and the ways that Success Academy generates cultural capital for its students), it is important to note that the families of the students we serve, be they on reservations or in cities, will always be a major source of power behind their children's academic success. We recognize that individuals without college degrees have other kinds of "knowledge and strengths" that educators do not have (Tierney 2000:223); thus their participation in Success Academy is critical. For this reason, we earnestly work toward engaging our students' relatives in their academic success through activities like maintaining a Success Academy web site and preparing news releases for hometown newspapers. We also take class pictures of the Success Academy freshmen, sophomores, juniors and seniors each academic year and mail these pictures to the students' homes during the summer. Enclosed is a letter from the Success Academy coordinator, describing the program of the past year and thanking family members for all the ways they support their children's educations.

Conclusion

Success Academy is not, first and foremost, a recruitment tool for South Dakota State University. But since the Success Academy program graduated its first students in 2004, 45 Flandreau Indian School students have enrolled at SDSU as concurrent students and 12 as true freshmen. Before the start of Success Academy, about one student per year attended SDSU after graduating from FIS.

Success Academy is a college preparatory program that serves children attending the Flandreau Indian School and living in the front yard of South Dakota State University. Just as importantly, Success Academy is an awareness and change project for South Dakota State University, a gift to SDSU from our neighbors at FIS.

By accepting this gift, SDSU will recruit more Native students into higher education, and it will retain those students through graduation. But this will only happen if "the priorities and core" of the university fundamentally change to accommodate "new voices and perspectives" (Hill 1991:45).

In the past, our business-as-usual methods of inviting Native American students to enter the gates of the university have presumed that these students will leave large parts of their identities parked outside. One need look no farther than our past numbers to see the failure of these approaches.

Our Success Academy partners at the Flandreau Indian School have been and continue to be giving and forgiving as we work together toward a better future for our children. I appreciate them for their patience and their faith. I also owe an enormous debt of gratitude to William G. Tierney (1993, 2000) and Julia E. Colyar (2006) for their thoughtful application of critical theory to college preparation programs (Tierney and Colyar 2006).

In summary, we must recognize difference within and between academic communities as a source of strength. Through prolonged involvement with diverse others we must learn what it means to truly honor individual identities. We must advocate, as does Tierney (2000:218), for giving Native students the cultural capital they need to succeed in the educational system as it currently exists, even while we work to reinvent the system that privileges some and excludes others on the basis of race and class. I offer the South Dakota State University-Flandreau Indian School Success Academy as an example of the power of community to affect the kind of fundamental changes I recommend.

Such fundamental changes will not happen overnight. The economic, cultural, spiritual and educational oppression suffered by indigenous people on this continent stretches back five centuries. The legacy of this oppression explains the underachievement of American Indians in higher education today. Those who are looking for quick jumps in Native college enrollment and giant leaps in American Indian retention will be disappointed.

Persistence is fundamental. Lakota spirituality reminds us to consider "not only what is good for today and tomorrow, but also what will be good for seven generations into the future" (Nichols and Nichols 1998:41). Today's Success Academy students include the seventh generation descendants of the Wounded Knee Massacre. In keeping with Lakota philosophy, the seventh generation is the one expected to bring healing and renewal.

SDSU-FIS Success Academy has just completed its seventh year. Recently I asked my 250 Success Academy colleagues, spread throughout South Dakota State University, this question: "What does SDSU gain from participating in the Success Academy program?" Here are some of their answers:

SDSU gains legitimate access to a relationship with a tribal school— its students, faculty and staff. We get to be a part of the creation of an exciting, informative school reform movement that appears to really be making a difference. SDSU gains the opportunity to learn about how to most effectively work with, educate and learn from our students at the Flandreau Indian School. —*An administrator*

I think SDSU gains a great deal from partnering with a minority high school. We gain insight into how American Indian students function in an academic setting and perhaps clues to help us be more welcoming and inclusive. As an SDSU teacher, I gain insight into better ways of teaching scientific material. Outreach is an important part of the role of a land grant university, and the partnership with the Flandreau Indian School is an important outreach activity. —*A professor*

A greater presence of Native students like those from FIS may help the university community as a whole to become friendlier and more conducive to Native peoples. —*A student*

SDSU gains an obvious and better insight into the needs and challenges facing the Flandreau Indian School and its students. We also gain an awareness of how we might better serve FIS and its students. It teaches us that one university, one group, even one individual can make a difference in the lives of students. —*A professional staff member*

These answers give me great hope. Collaboration with the Flandreau Indian School has opened up new ways of seeing and knowing for South Dakota State University administrators, faculty, staff and students. Our SDSU-FIS Success Academy partnership is truly a community built upon difference. As partners, we recognize that our differences in cultures are our source of strength. We are united by our desire to help more American Indian students prepare for and succeed in college.

The idea of building communities of difference was developed by critical theorist William G. Tierney. As Tierney and others maintain, a major shortcoming of critical theory is its separation from the real-life problems of individuals and the pursuit of social justice.

In our day-to-day Success Academy work, we try to model what it means to honor individual difference while working for societal good. Only by telling each other our stories, and by putting critical theory into practice, can we hope to create an equitable society in which all of our children are empowered to assume fruitful roles.

References:

Bourdieu, Pierre. 1977. "Cultural Reproduction and Social Reproduction." Pp. 487–511 in *Power and Ideology in Education*, edited by J. Karabel and A. H. Halsey. New York: Oxford University Press.

———. 1986. "The Forms of Capital." Pp. 241–258 in *Handbook of Theory and Research for the Sociology of Education*, edited by J. G. Richardson. New York: Greenwood Press.

Colyar, Julia E. 2006. "Neighborhood Academic Initiative: Connecting Culture and College Preparation." Pp. 39-56 in *Ethnicity Matters: Rethinking How Black, Hispanic and Indian Students Prepare for and Succeed in College*, edited by M. B. Lee. New York: Peter Lang.

Garrod, Andrew and Colleen Larimore, eds. 1997. *First Person, First Peoples: Native American College Graduates Tell Their Life Stories*. Ithaca, N.Y.: Cornell University Press.

Hill, Patrick J. 1991. "Multi-Culturalism: The Crucial Philosophical and Organizational Issues." *Change* 23(4):38-47.

King, Martin Luther, Jr. 1958. *Stride Toward Freedom: The Montgomery Story*. New York: Harper & Brothers.

Mehan, Hugh, Irene Villanueva, Lea Hubbard, and Angela Lintz. 1996. *Constructing School Success: The Consequences of Untracking Low-Achieving Students*. New York: Cambridge University Press.

Nichols, Laurie Stenberg and Tim Nichols. 1998. "2+2+2: Collaborating to Enhance Educational Opportunities for Native Americans." *Journal of Family and Consumer Sciences* 90:38–41.

Tierney, William G. 1993. *Building Communities of Difference: Higher Education in the Twenty-First Century*. Toronto, Ontario: OISE Press.

————. 2000. "Power, Identity and the Dilemma of College Student Departure." Pp. 213–234 in *Rethinking the Student Departure Puzzle*, edited by J. M. Braxton. Nashville: Vanderbilt University Press.

Tierney, William G. and Julia E. Colyar. 2006. *Urban High School Students and the Challenge of Access*. New York: Peter Lang.

Yosso, Tara J. 2005. "Whose Culture Has Capital? A Critical Race Theory Discussion of Community Cultural Wealth." *Race, Ethnicity and Education* 8:69–91.

Discussion Questions:

1. In what ways does ethnicity matter in the SDSU-FIS Success Academy program?

2. What factors contribute to making the SDSU-FIS Success Academy program successful?

3. What are the biggest obstacles that the SDSU-FIS Success Academy program faces?

3. How is the SDSU-FIS Success Academy program different from other programs that assist students of color in preparing for and succeeding in college?

Potluck Poetry and Prose: Women Writers Build Community on the Plains

Ruth Harper

Introduction

Linda Hasselstrom, South Dakota rancher, is also the award-winning author of eleven books, including *Feels Like Far*, *Land Circle*, *Windbreak*, and most recently, *Between Grass and Sky*. She is also co-editor of three anthologies of the writing of women who live in the high plains region. The third in the series, *Crazy Woman Creek: Women Rewrite the American West* (Houghton Mifflin, 2004), is a collection of women's writings about how women create community, connecting with each other as well as with a larger whole. The back cover copy says this book includes the voices of "153 women living west of the Mississippi" who describe "the ways women shape and sustain Western communities." Through screening hundreds of submissions and editing and assembling these anthologies, Hasselstrom has learned a great deal about how writing helps build community, particularly among women who live in this region.

In addition to writing, editing, and speaking on a variety of issues, Hasselstrom owns and operates Windbreak House, a retreat for women writers (or those who aspire to write). I participated in a writing retreat there during the summer of 2002 with my friend Ruby Wilson. It was an experience that encouraged, challenged, and somewhat daunted me. The setting is isolated, outside the small town of Hermosa, in western South Dakota.

From the deck of the house, I could see "Lake Linda," in that season a tiny pond, but alive to the discerning eye. (Linda has a most discerning eye, I quickly discovered.) In daylight, the Black Hills are visible in the far west, and after dark the entire gauzy galaxy is resplendent above.

The morning after my arrival, I woke to few distractions and no noise, not even the humming of an air conditioner. It was so hot that by the afternoon I imagined I could feel the inside of my brain sweat. But strangely, in the heat, quiet, and isolation, my head was clear, and I felt free to focus on writing about images, ideas, and experiences I'd carried around for some time: my adolescent daughter and her friends running through the house like wild ponies; the morning that fall arrived in Brookings riding the edge of a bracing cold front; the night my dying, adored father-in-law said goodbye to me in a sweat lodge dream.

Linda's generosity as a writing mentor is remarkable. She makes available all sorts of resources, but the primary force of creative energy is Linda herself. Residents write all day, sometimes responding to specific exercises or questions posed by the writer in residence, and meet in the cool of the evening to discuss what they have produced.

Linda is a tough, funny, and honest critic with a hearty, hooting laugh that makes one strive to elicit it again. She wears boots, even in the summer heat, and long cotton skirts that make her look as if she lived on that prairie before it was even surveyed. Her wardrobe is entirely practical and comfortable, and I felt a bit silly in my Capri pants and Doc Martens sandals. Before long, we were bra-less in tank tops, guzzling water all day and something stronger at night.

Evenings were haunted by the bizarre acrobatics of nighthawks, called thunderbirds by American Indians because of the unique, booming sounds the birds' wings produce when they dive, scooping up and gorging on miller moths. Sitting on the back deck, sipping whiskey, telling stories, and taking in the performance of the nighthawks is inspiration enough, but Linda makes her residents work.

Ruby, a Brookings, South Dakota, woman whose work has been included in two of the anthologies, has enjoyed three writing retreats at Windbreak House. Ruby says that Linda helps her and others "make a place in their lives for writing." She also notes that while "it can be difficult to have anyone evaluate my writing, . . . the end result is so much better with input from others" (Wilson, 1999, p.1). This sharing and seeking input from others is part of the community that women writers create.

When I first heard about SDSU colleagues producing a book about building and maintaining *community*, I was aware of only male contributors, great guys all (and scholars to boot). Still, I wondered, "no female perspective on community?" I soon discovered that two expressive women had, in fact, been included, but then I thought: how can there be a book about community building in the upper Midwest without the voices of *many* women? The idea of adding more voices of women to the collection led me straight (well, until I left the Interstate) to the door of Windbreak House and the wise woman within. Because I had spent three intense days working with Linda, when I interviewed her by e-mail I felt as if we were back on her deck, exchanging questions, answers, and laughter. I could taste the smoky whiskey, hear the pounding nighthawks, and occasionally be startled and pleased by her rollicking laugh.

RH: You've now put together three anthologies of the writings of women of the western or plains states. The first, *Leaning into the Wind*, shares the lives of rural women in the Western United States. The second, *Woven on the Wind*, describes relationships among women in the West. The third, *Crazy Woman Creek*, focuses on how these women influence community. Each collection has a different theme, but also some qualities in common with the others. How would you describe the similarities and differences among the three volumes?

LH: *Leaning into the Wind* was, I think, more spontaneous. More of the writers were inexperienced, and they scribbled their thoughts down without really believing their work would appear in a published book or that it would get so much attention. The lively casualness of those writings is unique and wonderful. For *Woven on the Wind* and *Crazy Woman Creek*, we received contributions from more experienced writers who had observed the popularity of the first book.

RH: Did one theme "out-draw" the others? Are women of this region especially eager to write about any particular topic?

LH: There are astonishing pieces in all three books, pieces which surprised us with the way the writers interpreted the theme, or expressed themselves, with the subject matter, or poignancy, or beauty, but the first book tapped a spring. Western women were amazed to find that someone cared about their lives enough to encourage them to write, and they responded with warmth and enthusiasm. I think we could go on publishing anthologies on the theme of life in the West almost indefinitely. Many women submitted stories about their lives for the next two books, believing the subjects were the same. We expected it to be more difficult for them to write about their friendships with women, and their participation in their communities, and it apparently was.

RH: Have several of the same women submitted work for all three volumes and, if so, have you seen them develop as writers over the years? In what ways and by what means do you see these women (and others) developing a sense of community or mutual support?

LH: Many of the same women submitted work for all three volumes. Writing by sixteen women (including the three editors) appears in all of the anthologies. And yes, we did observe an improvement in the writing of many. We definitely saw a rise in interest among Western women in writing as a result of the anthologies. Several women wrote to say that though we had rejected their work, they had gone on to write books, or family histories, or articles, and they thanked us for inspiring them. We also know of at least one anthology, inspired by our first call for manuscripts, that was collected from a particular region of one state. And the women continue to develop mutual support and community by showing up for readings, notifying us of their successes, encouraging each other by mail and e-mail. I believe many of them have realized through the community of the books that other women are interested in the same issues, and they are more willing to write their views, or speak out in their local areas, because of the validation of the books.

I said to a friend recently that I wasn't much of an activist for women's rights. She responded: "I see the anthologies . . . as activist acts. Marching and protesting doesn't feel right to me here and now. But . . . giving print to so many voices that otherwise might not get into print, and offering them as a collection so that their collective voices are so powerful—that, to me, is a positive stand for the human spirit. If it's not activism, how would you describe it?"

RH: It sounds as if some lasting, nurturing relationships have been built through the creation of your anthologies. I know you have written of "the comfortable ordinariness" and the "spirit of hope and bond of love" you found in these writings (Hasselstrom, 2001, p. xviii). These would appear to be a strong foundation for enduring friendship.

LH: Not only have the editors become closer, more intimate friends as a result of the work, but we've each built strong friendships with contributors. One woman whom I accepted to a retreat at Windbreak House on the basis of her writing for the anthology has returned to write with me every year since we met. She and another contributor were already on retreat at Windbreak House when my mother died, and went to the funeral with me. We are more than writer and students now.

RH: It occurs to me that Western or pioneer women built community in the past through writing letters, journaling, and perhaps through creating hymns or church-related poetry. How does that compare to women writers on the plains today? Do these women's voices currently have other outlets? Where do you see or hear the stories of women's lives told in our society? Have your anthologies given voice to women who might otherwise be silent or unheard?

LH: I think the anthologies provide the same kinds of connections as our pioneer mothers developed, though today's e-mail contacts probably outnumber meetings at the quilt rack and church social. That doesn't mean we shouldn't also meet face to face, but the e-mail and other contacts may facilitate more personal exchanges. Today's connections probably span greater distances. A pioneer woman who left her family and friends in New York to travel west might never see them again, and exchange only a few letters a year. Now a woman who moves here from the East can keep in constant contact and can share opinions on news while it's happening. Surely this encourages women to speak out, to recognize our similarity with each other, and to act on our beliefs.

Women probably have more outlets today—e-mail, for example— but the anthologies last, can be read and re-read, and that allows time for reflection, reconsideration, expansion of ideas. Rural women, often more isolated, may benefit more from the connections formed by the books since they often spend less time actually seeing other people than do their urban sisters. I think it is particularly those rural women, many of whom do not have e-mail or even good regular telephone service, who may benefit most–because they are often ignored or missed when writers are talking about the ways Americans live. I'm pleased that more Western women are being published generally today; that's a good sign, and the anthologies have both encouraged and been part of this trend. Western women get more attention in news features now, too, and are part of a general trend toward increased participation by women in public life. But many of those opportunities haven't been readily available to rural women, or perhaps weren't attractive to them—so yes, we have helped many be heard who otherwise might not have been.

RH: Some of the writers in your anthologies seem to have to write, and must be pleased to have these books help put their words before the public, joined with those of others. In a chapter introduction in *Woven* (2001), you and Gaydell Collier quote your contributors in saying that

> . . . "poetry is the rutted road" we must follow. Stories keep us from going "crazier than a rat in a coffee can" and remind us that "we don't go alone," that "communication is the road to sanity." Besides preserving experiences, these stories teach us that "women's journeys are more alike than not" and that we all share the "blood language of this

place." If we met our foremothers, our "callused hands would reach" to touch each other as our words have done. (p. 199)

LH: Each phrase in the introductions to the divisions of the book is quoted from the writing of one of the contributors to the book. Yet when the piece is read, all those phrases from different women blend into a seamless whole, as if one woman was speaking. I find this remarkable, even now, since each woman took an entirely different approach to her subject. But the subject of the entire book was relationships among women, and perhaps this demonstrates metaphorically that no matter what our differences, we are much more alike than we are different.

RH: Why are these books important? What do you believe your anthologies contribute to literature and/or American culture?

LH: These anthologies are important because they are the REAL voices of contemporary Western women talking about their truths, not myths imposed by someone else. Their truths don't always agree, but they all deserve to be heard. We're delighted to see these books read by book clubs or individuals, in college courses—maybe all this effort will help put some of the old Western myths to sleep, permanently. Women have thanked me for writing in a way that shows that they have thoughts beyond the welfare of the cows; that not all of us wear boots and hats; that we are all not size 10; that men do not necessarily run everything here, and on and on.

All three editors are members of various professional organizations, and we've all done some modest promoting within various circles of readers. Watching discussion lists of academicians, I've been a little frustrated by the lack of discussion of these books by teachers who seem more interested in blockbuster novels by popular writers who aren't nearly as real, or as knowledgeable about the West, as these women. But acceptance takes time, and I hope that more and more teachers, especially, will see these books as the terrific resources they are. For one thing, these women are ALIVE! They are scattered all over the region. You, the professor, in some small college without the funds to pay for a visit by that blockbuster writer so much in demand on televised talk shows, could invite the woman from the next county or town and she'd be delighted to speak to your class about reality in the West. She may not cite the authorities in the field, but she speaks from experience from which our students seem more distant every year.

RH: What is unique about the perspectives of women writers in this geographic region? How does the landscape, or the weather, or other environmental aspects of the West, influence their writing?

LH: These women's perspectives are as unique as the West, which is to say that of course we share some characteristics with women in other regions, just as some other parts of the country have high winds. But in every way, the West is unique, and so are the people who live here. The West is full of contradictions, and Western women seem to respond differently than Eastern women to similar situations. Here's an anecdote that proves the point (also recounted in the introduction to *Crazy Woman Creek*): What would the Devils Tower publication celebration of *Leaning into the Wind* have been like had it been held in Boston? Our East Coast editor replied, "less open, less warm. The women would have worn less comfortable shoes and tried to stand by the most important person."

RH: Very funny! I prefer comfortable shoes myself and can never figure out who is really most important. Do you see influences of Native American cultures in the writing of women in the plains?

LH: Yes, in all kinds of subtle ways, besides the fact that more Native Americans are being published in all sorts of venues where they haven't appeared before. I also think many Western women would agree with the Native American idea that feminism is irrelevant to them—because they were BORN liberated.

I find evidence of the way non-Native women are aware of, and influenced by, Native cultures in many of the submissions we received for the books, particularly *Crazy Woman Creek*. I'm not sure if I'm remembering submissions that were accepted for publication or not, but a number of writers mention going on isolated retreats and speak of vision quests. There are a number, both in and not in the books, who use the talking stick idea. Also, there are many references to the power of the circle. One circle in *Woven* uses talking sticks, burden baskets, giveaway baskets, all as part of ritual. Some of these writers' ideas seem to be interwoven with goddess symbols, images, celebrations, and rites, so I can't say precisely what the origins of the ideas are. And while many Native Americans might argue that Whites should not adopt these practices, it is clear that many women are trying to do so in a respectful manner, trying to learn from their elders, to reconnect to ideas and philosophies that preceded White settlement in an effort to learn how to live more responsibly. And of course, some Whites who try to write about Native culture do so badly and in a way that is exploitive—but that's true any time ideas move through a population.

RH: What do you see as the key motivations for the women writers you have worked with—are they seeking validation?

LH: Many speak of validation: their belief in the power of their own stories has been increased because the rest of the world has taken notice now, in part through these books. They have confidence in their ability to deal with the world, but many of them feel that they are not respected; the prevalence of the Western myths about both women and men are demeaning. I've noticed this in responses to my own work as well. Western women want to record the true stories of the region, so people in other areas can know the reality; they want to be part of American culture as they really are, not as thin, made-up figures on a movie screen.

RH: Your comments call to mind another passage in *Reimagining Windbreak House* (2001) in which you write about your urge to support rural women writers in learning to cherish their perspectives and contributions:

> In my travels, I'd often encountered the belief that rural life and hard work are synonymous with ignorance. I'd also met dozens of women

who wanted to write but had been discouraged by officious teachers in high school or college. I could sympathize, having been told by a professor in graduate school I should go back to the ranch, get married, and have babies, because I wasn't smart enough for advanced education. Women who read my published work sometimes thanked me for telling *their* stories, for showing, as one said, "that ranch women aren't just big dumb cows." If I could encourage these women to write about their lives, could show them their stories had value, I might help them live more satisfying lives, and add their important viewpoints to our culture and history. (pp. 78-79)

LH: Those remain some of the primary reasons for working so hard on the anthologies.

RH: What surprised you most about the stories, essays, and poems you have read—both those included and those not included in your anthologies?

LH: Perhaps most surprising was the beauty and power of writing from women with little or no training, their ability to be articulate and eloquent on the subjects important to them. We knew they had these feelings and thoughts, but not that they would express themselves so well.

RH: I agree. As you say in *Woven on the Wind,* (2001):

When distance, circumstance, or death separates us from a friend, our "hearts travel on trails of tears and love and laughter." We feel our friends' influence "like the silent steel ribbons connecting the railways across the plains, helping drive us forward." In "one deep and universal breath," the words . . . offer solace, teaching us that "some days rays of laughter" can bridge "the ache of distance." Separate and yet together, we listen as the "wind brings their voices," the leaves whispering quietly, subtle as the blue-green hues of sagebrush. (p. 106)

LH: I could not have written that passage by myself, but all our voices joined to make it one smooth and lovely whole: community in action.

RH: And turning to other types of community, I've noticed that both book groups and all kinds of writing are flourishing these days. Why do you believe this is happening?

LH: Maybe people are ready again for the tangibility of the book, the trustworthiness of the written word, a more permanent record. Many have been inspired to write their own stories instead of watching someone else's story go by. This is kind of an interesting aside, but we three editors of the anthologies were ourselves a prize for a book club at a book festival in Denver a couple of years ago. The winning book group got to meet with us and ask us questions, and they loved it. *Crazy Woman Creek* has a reader's guide bound right into it. Houghton Mifflin, the publisher, must realize that book groups are an important element of the market these days.

RH: I shared your comments with my friend Nan Steinley, also a writer and member of a book group I'm in, who said:

> I like Linda's response about the tangibility of the book, a more permanent record. And writing one's own story instead of (or in addition to) reading only the stories of others. I think there's some sort of inherent need for many to write their own stories, not necessarily even to share with others, but to capture one's presence and place. I write, at times, so I don't forget myself in the weighty press of every single day. Some days go by and I've nothing to show for having lived it. For me writing at some level captures that I was here and this is what I and perhaps others did, said, heard, felt, saw. (personal communication, May 25, 2004)

LH: Your friend Nan? Nan Steinley and I were acquainted years ago, but haven't seen each other for—what? Thirty years? But we agree completely on this. I find it significant that two women with widely divergent lives have developed precisely the same ideas about the importance of writing in their lives.

RH: Since attending the writing retreat at Windbreak House, Ruby Wilson and I have met once a month to share and critique each other's writing. Ruby commented that "book and writing groups . . . give me a sense of value and strength that I don't find in other groups" (personal communication, December 17, 2003). How do you see women build community through writing?

LH: Women definitely build community through writing by writing with one another, reading one another's work, reading the same books and talking about them, even writing letters and e-mails—all part of the same connections. It's hard to evaluate just how broad this influence may be, because I've remained in one region most of my life. I've most often found women to be more helpful than competitive here, though I've heard horror stories about competition and back-stabbing. I hope we are helping each other more than competing; writing isn't a contest, despite the appearance in the marketplace. It's the writing that is important, and if I damage another writer, my writing is not improved.

RH: Do rural women relate to one another differently than urban women? How does the social structure of rural society affect the writing of women in small towns, on farms and ranches?

LH: I think rural women relate to one another differently than their urban sisters, in part because they see each other less often—but the books are a long answer to this question. Rural women may be less inclined to exchange confidences on intimate personal matters than urban women, and particularly so in contrast to young urban women. We editors have occasionally been shocked speechless at questions or comments about matters we don't discuss with one another, despite our long friendship. But the support of rural women for one another in times of hardship is strong; they may not talk about the tragedy, but they bring a potluck dish.

My first personal experience of this came when my husband died; few of the older women in my community hugged me or said anything personal. But as I was going through the line for the post-funeral lunch—an occasion I wanted desperately to miss–I started looking in their eyes. Their faces were brimming with love and concern, and knowledge. Every one of them was a widow, and they knew, as my contemporaries did not, what I was suffering.

We've seen similar responses at the celebrations for the anthologies as well. A widowed woman who chose to stay on the family farm was approached by other new widows who had not yet decided what to do; they formed an instant support group. Yet unless we know we have something in common, and receive encouragement, rural women are usually reluctant to speak about difficult matters—alcoholism, abuse, drug use. Because of our silence, some folks still think bad things can't happen in rural neighborhoods.

RH: This reminds me of your essay in *Between Earth and Sky* (2002) called "The Pot of Hospitality Still Simmers." Your anthologies could easily be compared to a potluck feast, in which the three-bean salad Sandra brings will appeal to some guests, while others will prefer Diane's traditional Jello with canned fruit. Those concerned about health may actually eat some of Milly's broccoli with cheese sauce, but most will skip it to leave room for Polly's pumpkin pie, or Mavis's mince, or Sally's fresh strawberry. (p. 64)

You also note that "guests may be brought together by interests rather than proximity, creating the kind of communities our ancestors knew" (p. 65).

LH: Now that I've become a bit more electronically savvy, and have a web site, I am frequently drawn into discussions with women all over the nation on our interests, our political views, our fears and problems. People astonish me with the connections they find. One year when I attended the Cowboy Poetry Gathering in Elko, Nevada, I kept noticing a tiny Asian woman smiling at me. I finally introduced myself, and asked her how she came to attend. She had come to meet me! Brought up in a traditional

Chinese community in San Francisco, she felt a deep kinship with me through my writing, and wanted to see me; that's all–she didn't want us to correspond, but she wanted to see if I matched her picture of me. Few of our foremothers had such opportunities.

RH: That's so true. How have other women encouraged or discouraged your writing? How do you feel about becoming a mentor, model, and source of encouragement for so many women who write? How has your literary success affected your writing and your ability to support other women in their writing?

LH: My earliest mentors were women English teachers in high school, and I've followed their example. I'm delighted to encourage other women, through the anthologies, through teaching workshops in various places, and by running my writing retreat just for women. My belief in the importance of my writing is enhanced when I see that my example encourages other women. My literary success has made me more visible, so other women are more likely to see me as a role model, which makes me a little nervous, since of course I've made plenty of visible mistakes! But I'm happy that a combination of circumstances allows me to keep the Windbreak House retreat going, even though it doesn't pay its way as well as a business should.

On the other hand, my upbringing also included plenty of women, among them my mother, who did not consider writing a profession. She didn't really want me to have a profession; she wanted me to marry a lawyer and have babies. To the end of her days, she never ceased asking if I'd gotten a job yet! In similar ways, other women (and men) around me discouraged me from writing; commenting snidely on my choice to return to my father's name after I was divorced; remarking that it was too bad I wasted my college education since I "ended up" back on the ranch shoveling manure. Some have suggested that my life is worthless because I haven't reproduced, others that I am clearly uninterested in community since I don't belong to clubs or a church. I know that many women even today do not see the writer as serving a valuable role in society, so I think it's important to be counted as a woman who does not necessarily follow a traditional role, to offer that example to younger women. I find it most intriguing, given my outspoken stances and nontraditional ways, that the Girl Scouts of the Black Hills are giving me an award in 2004 as a "woman of distinction," and therefore role model for Girl Scouts.

RH: I can't help but wonder what your mother would think of that award! Can you say more about how success has affected your writing and your ability to encourage other women to write?

LH: Success is a double-edged sword. I get more letters from women who want me to encourage them, more requests for speeches, more awards—but every one of those things takes time away from my own writing. I chose working with women at writing retreats as the most useful thing I could do for other women with the least damage to my own work—but so far I can't survive on the income from those retreats. So I must accept other jobs, and the frustration that goes with them.

RH: I appreciated your sharing with me recent research on women and stress management, because I see connections between that research (e.g., women tend and befriend in order to cope) and the ways women support each other's writing efforts at your retreats. The authors of *Best Friends: The Pleasures and Perils of Girls' and Women's Friendships* (1998) note that when women become overwhelmed with their responsibilities, they tend to neglect the friendships that nurture them. They say that women need unpressured space in order to connect with other women in ways that sustain and help them.

LH: I agree that many women respond in this way to pressure, so part of my work at Windbreak House is to educate the women who come there *not* to do that. My focus is writing, and its importance in our lives, but the house is a metaphor for the way women who treat each other as friends can help each other focus on whatever is important to them. When I began the retreats, I didn't think that I would be creating new friendships;

I wanted to help women become writers. But I soon realized that the two effects are in some cases interdependent, so I certainly don't work against the formation of friendships.

RH: When I think of Windbreak House, I recall exactly that rare experience of *unpressured space*. It is there both in the topography of land that stretches uncluttered for miles in all directions, but also in the supportive acceptance that women who meet there guarantee themselves and each other, with your assistance. Your anthologies also provide space and build community, not only among women writers on the plains, but also among readers, those who value the insight, pathos, and humor found in the places you've created and nurtured. Thank you so much for sharing your valuable time to reflect with me and to share insights based on your experiences as a writer.

LH: I try to be thoughtful about my choices. Responding to this interview, for example, has taken as much time as writing a short essay but your questions have helped me, too, by making me examine my place in the world. You've given me new ideas to reflect on, new perspectives. And that's how I try to make anything that is not writing function: as a challenge that enhances the work I've chosen to do.

One way of building community is by accepting challenges, turning them into tools with which to create something new. So our friendship has grown closer because we have exchanged ideas and information by way of the interview tool. I find that very satisfying. And this work we've done has created a web between us—stronger than if I'd been working in isolation on my own writing, while you worked in isolation on yours.

Conclusion

Reviewing my experience at Windbreak House and the body of Linda Hasselstrom's work, I realize that her words regarding friendship are powerfully true. The immense gift of an artist's time is undeniably the gift of unique friendship. I have learned so much from Linda despite amazingly little direct contact. Perhaps the most important lesson I have taken is that of aspiring to expressing myself more creatively. Because I so highly esteem good writing, I often feel incapable of doing it myself. Linda's acceptance of my presence at Windbreak House meant a great deal to me. Her conviction that my personal reflections and observations could be crafted into verbal images worth saving, sharing, deconstructing, or even publishing was more than encouraging; it was contagious.

From the high hill of middle age, I now can see that what I might leave to my children, my friends, my students, or others might include crystallized memories, lessons, or insights put into words. And, as someone has said, an image in a poem is like being alive twice. Through writing, I can re-experience the intricate relationships nurtured in a thriving twelve-year-old book group or the astonishing impact of my eighteen-year-old daughter's sassy wisdom. Through Linda's writing, I learned things about widowhood that both terrified and buffered me through my husband's recent cancer surgery.

When I began this interview project on the topic of women building community through writing, I had no idea that I would participate in the publication party for *Crazy Woman Creek* in May, 2004. As I sat among those writers, I truly wondered what I was doing there. In fact, I felt as if there were a giant neon sign on my forehead flashing "fraud." As the first women read aloud their poems and essays, I was astounded at how little their appearances suggested the depth of their passions. In tears, Nancy Kile spoke of her "White face and Lakota heart" (p. 46). Christine Valentine, in her formal yet fading British accent, told of driving down gravel roads and finding community through selling Avon products until the commissions were reduced to the point that she lost money (p. 166). Kathleen Gotschall made us laugh with a joke about the difference between a rodeo mom and a pit bull: lipstick (p.177). And my friend Ruby described the two lilac bushes she sees on her evening walks, "with about enough room between them for a small house" (p. 25). Bernie Koller (p. 133) and Emilie Hoppe (p. 232) gave contrasting portraits of living in religious colonies. Sophie Dominik Echeverria (p. 202) taught us all to do the Basque ululation, which they may still be talking about in downtown Chadron. Someday Sophie will write a marvelous story about *that*.

Women in this region *do* build community through writing. It is one way we explore one another's souls and hold each other up. Through simple, friendly e-mails and modern versions of what used to be called bread-and-butter notes, as well as poetry, essays, and stories, we share the lives we lead and bring our best dishes to the table.

References:

Apter, T., Josselson, R., & Baron, J. (1998). *Best Friends: The Pleasures and Perils of Girls' and Women's Friendships*. New York: Crown Publishing Group.

Hasselstrom, L.M. (2002). *Between grass and sky: Where I live and work*. Reno: University of Nevada Press.

Hasselstrom, L.M. (2001, Winter). *Reimagining windbreak house*. Michigan Quarterly Review, XL, 1, 74-90.

Hasselstrom, L.M., Collier, G., & Curtis, N. (Eds.). (2001). *Woven on the wind: Women write about friendship in the sagebrush west*. New York, NY: Houghton Mifflin Co.

Roripaugh, L.A. (2001). Poet of the wind: An interview with Linda Hasselstrom. *South Dakota Review*, 39, pp. 7-26.

Wilson, R. (1999, Autumn). Windbreak house gives writers new perspective. *Arts Alive South Dakota*, 1.

Discussion Questions:

1. How do you make space in your life for personal activities that are important to you?

2. How do you engage with or support others who might share that interest? What sort of sense of community has emerged from this sharing?

3. If you are a writer, how do you sustain motivation and inspiration? How do you give and receive feedback on writing?

4. After reading this interview, how has your thinking about women supporting other women or writers supporting other writers changed or not changed?

Images of Community

One of the archetypal elements of human existence, "community" is a phenomenon that cannot be captured in a single word or phrase, nor can it be subsumed in a particular image or even a bundle of images. But it can be pointed to; it can be evoked from a variety of perspectives. Its various aspects can be referenced so long as we allow that it is multifaceted and often vague, contradictory, and ineffable as well. The photographic image provides a useful complement to the spoken word in assisting us in our attempt to capture the notion of community.

"We can usually tell at a glance what a photograph is about," cultural historian Alan Trachtenberg notes. "But the image does not always tell us everything we want to know." Somewhere between the hard facts captured by the camera and the imaginative response of the viewer lie truths about community that can help us better understand what it is all about.

1. Community lay at the heart of the cultures of the first people on the land—the American Indians—and it remains there today. Drummers, singers, and dancers perform traditional songs at a wacipi in South Dakota State University's Frost Arena in 2000. (SDSU University Relations)

2. Associate Professor Chuck Tiltrum helps Tanessa Wescogame spot a target with a tripod level at a Flandreau Indian School Success Academy workshop at South Dakota State University in 2001. SDSU, like some other schools, has been working to integrate American Indian students into the higher education community in recent years. (SDSU University Relations)

3. Flandreau Indian School students dine with professors and mentors as they learn the ins and outs of the college scene at South Dakota State University. Heirs of centuries of tribal community traditions, Native Americans are now finding ways to participate in other community activities and institutions. (Richard Lee)

4. Unlike their Native American predecessors in the region, European-Americans began constructing large commercial edifices in their communities. Small-town grain elevators were magnets drawing farmers together to discuss crops, the weather, politics, and sports teams. Federal Farm Security Administration photographer John Vachon captured this group of kibitzers in Bowdle, South Dakota, on a Saturday afternoon in 1942. (South Dakota State Historical Society)

5. The land not only provided the physical and economic basis for early communities. Containing a rich variety of flora and fauna, it also constituted a complex biological community itself. Author Linda Hasselstrom, who conducts writing workshops at her ranch bordering on the Black Hills, continues to write eloquently about the land and its relationship to community. (Ruby Wilson)

6. Hundreds of abandoned homes and farmsteads dotting the rural landscape stand as mute testimony to the vibrant family and community life that once blanketed the region. Today, community has become more spread out as it faces new challenges and opportunities. (Ruby Wilson)

7. Early homesteaders depended heavily upon neighbors and community residents, both to get their work done and to participate with in recreational activities. Local farmers volunteered their labor to raise a barn in the expectation that those they assisted would reciprocate when they needed help themselves. (Miner County Historical Society)

8. Threshing runs were an integral part of early community life. While men and boys sweated and strained pitching bundles outside, women and girls prepared hearty meals inside for the men when they came in for lunch. German immigrants south of Howard, South Dakota, pose for the photographer before 1900. (Miner County Historical Society)

139

9. Hundreds of small towns sprang up quickly to accommodate the needs of farmers in the surrounding countryside. During the early 1940s, you could get a good meal for only 35 cents at the air-conditioned Tourist Café on Main Street in Kadoka, South Dakota. (South Dakota Agricultural Heritage Museum)

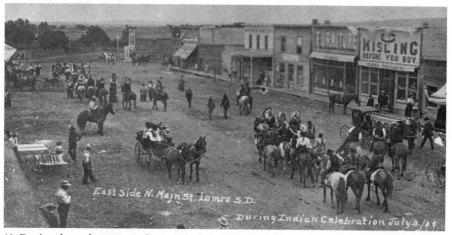

10. During the early 1900s, Indians and whites joined together to celebrate Independence Day in dozens of small towns on the plains. When July 4 fell on a Sunday, as it did here in Lamro, South Dakota, in 1909, the celebration would take place on Saturday. (South Dakota Agricultural Heritage Museum)

11. The strong sense of community that existed in early small towns always heightened when the nation went to war. In Brookings, hundreds of townspeople show up to wish the young men in Company C godspeed in September 1917, as they head off to the training camps. (George Norby Collection)

12. On market days—especially on Saturday nights—people drove in from all around to meet with friends and neighbors on small-town main streets. There aren't many empty parking spaces on Winner's brightly-lit Main Street in this 1940s scene. (South Dakota State Historical Society)

13. The Palace Hotel and Café in White, South Dakota (shown in 2007), is one of the many kinds of "third places" that bring people together and where community is played out in its most elemental form. (Richard Lee)

14. Anybody who doesn't know what's going on in the community after attending morning coffee hour (as here at Jimmy's Café in Clear Lake, South Dakota, in 2001) simply isn't paying very close attention. (SDSU Journalism Department)

15. Community centers, such as this one in White, South Dakota, bring people together to visit, relax, recreate, and do the community's business. (Richard Lee)

16. The Northern Plains have been home to some of the most active communitarians in the United States. Fraternal lodges and sororities, ladies aids, service clubs, and other community groups, while somewhat less active today than they used to be, continue to thrive. The Pythian Sisters Lodge of Pierre pose for the photographer around 1910. (South Dakota State Historical Society)

17. Many organizations and activities have brought children and adults and people of all social groups and characteristics together through the years. This colorful group of actors pose for a picture in the Couse Opera House in De Smet, South Dakota, in 1912. (South Dakota State Historical Society)

18. Children participate in outdoor drills in May 1918 in Brookings by carrying American flags. The Young Citizens League emerged soon afterwards to foster patriotism, civic responsibility, and democratic values in students. (South Dakota Agricultural Heritage Museum)

19. Girls and boys march around the Maypole in Brookings in 1918. Note the hats and dressed-up clothing. Schools were centers of community in towns and on the countryside. (South Dakota Agricultural Heritage Museum)

20. For towns like Rutland (population: 20+), the presence of a school continues to symbolize the health and strength of community. Countless memories inhabit the hallways of this classic two-story brick structure built in 1921 that houses 110 students, many of whom transfer into the district because of the school's quality. (Richard Lee)

21. Volunteer firefighters gather together in Pierre. The highest levels of volunteerism, an essential element of community, have been recorded on the Northern Plains. (South Dakota State Historical Society)

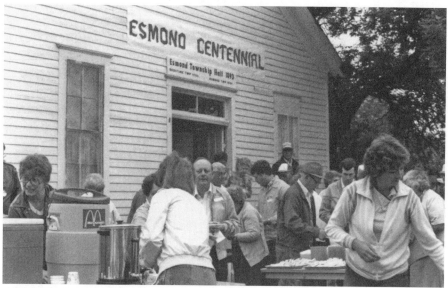

22. More than 700 people showed up to celebrate the centennial of tiny Esmond (population: 6) in 1985. Community continues to carry on in memory in places like this, even after most of the inhabitants have moved on. (John Miller)

23. Play, as much as work, grounds community. People of all ages enjoyed swimming at Twin Lakes, south of Roswell, during the 1930s. The dance hall on the left was likewise the site of a lot of action and excitement. (Miner County Historical Society)

24. In death, as in life, community bonds people together. A horse-drawn hearse leads a funeral procession to the gravesite at Dalesburg in Clay County, South Dakota, during the early 1900s. (South Dakota Agricultural Heritage Museum)

25. There are many paths to community and many ways to negotiate the journey. The more aware people are of the importance and necessity of community, the more likely they will be to fulfill their desire to be part of community. (Ruby Wilson)

26. Community begins in the land, and its ultimate viability depends on the natural environment from which it emerges. Just like all life forms, community requires cultivation and care. At the end of the day, the quality of our lives is a derivative of the communities in which we live. (Ruby Wilson)

Her Words:
Linda Hasselstrom
Reads at Augustana

Ruth Harper

Her keen eyes snap and shine,
head tilts
like the birds she observes so closely
on sprawling plains
and in clapboard Cheyenne.

She is mindfully awake,
attentive to the pacific grace of grasslands;
alert to their understated dramas—
    kettles of hawks,
    exhaltations of larks,
    medleys of wildflowers;
her vigilance constant
as a hovering kestrel
alive with vivid, heedful language
as the rest of us drink lattés
and neglect to look up.

Energy springs from her toes,
streams out her hair;
hands that know how to work cattle also

dance elegantly with words,
   rise with the night heron,
   hail curious neighbors.
Her well-worn boots stride abandoned cemeteries.

She is the solitary mourner
at eroded gravestones,
a stranger's infant daughters,
prairie lambs long forgotten.

She ponders whether her parents,
resting elsewhere in this clay,
understand at last
that words are her beloved children.

Going Once, Going Twice

Ruby R. Wilson

The auctioneer's voice drones on
as he backs and sidesteps
toward the last item.
He already sold Granny's quilts,
and the antique oval frames
that Mom put on the trailer
with the pictures still in them.

"Start it up!" the auctioneer commands.
My brother steps in, turns the key.
I hear the familiar low rumble,
the slow grating of the augers,
sieves, straw walkers.
Memories crowd in
of tan summer days,
fluid fields of musky wheat.

Every May, Dad loaded this Massey Ferguson
Super 92 combine on a trailer,
hitched to the Dodge truck.
Our family faced the warm wind
to Mountain View, Oklahoma
from South Dakota. We worked
our way back north, custom harvesting
winter wheat as we traveled.

I was sixteen when I learned to drive the truck
on the rolling white clay roads
near Kensington, Kansas.
Creaking up the first hill
I missed the rhythm of the shift.
Ten tons of wheat and I wallowed
backward, to the bottom of the hill.

The next year I learned how to
unload on the go,
match the speed of the truck
to the combine as it harvested
and unloaded grain into the truck box.
None was wasted.

Dad was amazed that I could hear
the quiet knocking of the damaged rod bearing
in the truck engine. He had it repaired
before more damage was done.
I drove the old '57 Dodge in the meantime
that took its half of the road out of the middle,
wandered from side to side
as I herded it down I-90
into Chamberlain, South Dakota.

In a tank top, jeans and harness boots,
I could tarp a truck,
and back it up square to a grain auger at a bin.
I wondered if the chivalrous elevator hand
who took the shovel from me
to clean out the corners of the truck box
helped his pregnant wife
lug the laundry or mop the floors.

Nights on the road
I would lie awake in the top bunk
of the camper, parked at a truck stop
somewhere along the highway, listen
to faint music drift across the gravel lot
lit by neon lights.

The bidding ends.
Strangers that I grew up with
who know my name and relatives
claim the treasures, discuss our family later
around their kitchen tables.

Discussion Questions:

1. How do auctions play a role in the life of the community?

2. What is the speaker saying about the relationship between this family
   and the community?

The Ups and Downs of Community in Clear Lake in Recent Years

John E. Miller

The crises of depression and war, which threatened the very survival of democracy and the capitalist economic order and which in some ways undermined social solidarity, ultimately stimulated an even stronger sense of community. But one of the casualties of the massive social and economic changes that occurred in the United States during the decades after World War II was the tight sense of community that had prevailed previously. By the 1960s, under the influence of the Vietnam War, the civil rights revolution, the women's rights movement, and a myriad of other wrenching social changes and conflicts, social cohesion came under challenge in unprecedented ways. Conflict became as common as consensus, and people questioned whether we would ever be able to recapture a sense of common purpose.

The sixties earned a reputation as an age of hedonism, characterized by the rise of the New Left and the counter-culture. Critics labeled the years following it the "Me Decade" and "the culture of narcissism" and worried that the notion of community, with its accompanying sense of duty and obligation, was being overshadowed by the rise of self-expressive individualism. The Reagan years and after witnessed further manifestations of the breakdown of community. In 2000, Harvard sociologist Robert Putnam captured attention with *Bowling Alone: The Collapse and Revival of American Community*, a book that argued that, starting in the 1960s, the spirit of community seriously eroded in the United States. He lamented the reduced connections uniting individuals and the decline of "social capital," by which he meant the "social networks and the norms of reciprocity and trustworthiness" that arise from those social connections.

Putnam's memorable title derived from his observation that Americans were frequenting bowling alleys more than ever before but that increasingly they were bowling alone rather than in organized leagues. Such leagues had emerged gradually in the United States during the 1920s, had grown during the Depression Decade, had dropped slightly during the war years, and then had exploded in the two decades after World War II, before declining continuously after the mid-1960s. In Putnam's book, "bowling alone" served as a metaphor for the way in which organizational activity of all types—fraternal groups, service and volunteer organizations, Parent-Teacher Associations, Scouting, 4-H, political parties, and other similar entities—went into decline after 1960.

For Putnam and a growing number of observers, this decline in social capital, civic virtue, public-spiritedness, or community—call it what you will—presents a serious problem for the future of our society and political democracy. Putnam isolated four major factors behind the decline in civic engagement: pressures of time and money, notably the challenge of two-career families; suburbanization, with its accompanying sprawl and increased commuting; the rise of electronic entertainment, especially in the form of television; and, most importantly, generational change. The younger generation, it turns out, is much less civically involved than was the World War II generation.

Interestingly, Putnam noted that the kinds of things that undergird social capital, such as honesty, trustworthiness, altruism, philanthropy, community service, volunteerism, and the willingness to give directions to strangers, remain more common in small towns than in more urbanized areas. No region of the country ranks higher on the scale than the Upper Midwest and Great Plains. At the top of the list are the two Dakotas. In seeking to explain this condition, Putnam suggested that it has something to do with such things as migration patterns, Scandinavian population concentrations, high levels of educational attainment and child development, low levels of television viewing, and other social factors, but he provided no definite answer to the question.

If Putnam's observations are correct, small towns in the Midwest and the Great Plains can take some comfort from them, while at the same time having reason to be concerned. On the one hand, the evidence suggests that small rural towns retain a stronger sense of civic participation and community spirit than do more metropolitan regions. On the other hand, they are also very much a part of the drift of the times, experiencing all of the social forces that undermine community, including two-career families, the expansion of the electronic media, and pressures of time and money. Holding on to older practices of neighborliness and community interaction, while at the same time recognizing the need to accommodate themselves to new social and economic realities, creates tension in the lives of small town-residents. How they choose to react to these challenges will play a crucial role in the quality of life that they will enjoy.

Clear Lake, South Dakota, a typical small town in the region, retained a strong sense of community during the Great Depression and World War II years, but struggled with the forces unleashed in rural areas after World War II. Those forces included increased farm size and a declining rural population, competition from large corporations and chain stores, declining numbers of locally-owned stores, the exodus of young people, an aging population base, the rise of two wage-earner families, the proliferation of the mass media, and declining membership in traditional groups and organizations. It is clear, however, that in many ways, while pressures continue to mount on people's time and resources, a strong sense of community persists in Clear Lake, contributing measurably to the quality of life its residents enjoy.

The first thing that would probably strike a Rip Van Winkle who slept during the last several decades is the large transformation that has occurred in Clear Lake's economy. Where once there were four hardware stores and four groceries, now only one of each remains. Six gas stations have been reduced to three, three pharmacies to one. New on the scene are two convenience stores, one of which rents VCR and DVD movies, which people now watch in the privacy of their homes. The Majestic Theatre, built in 1930 and thereafter the focus of a great deal of community activity, closed its doors in the late 1960s after Main Street businesspeople had volunteered considerable time and money to try to keep it open.

Gone, too, are a men's store and a department store, although a women's boutique and gift shop continues to provide enough unique merchandise and service to attract customers from as far away as Sioux Falls, Aberdeen, and even Minneapolis. In addition, the town boasts four utilities companies and insurance offices, and two each of banks, law offices, realtors, lumberyards, beauty shops, electricians, and—most surprisingly—automobile dealerships. Other businesses include an abstract company, a bakery, a data systems provider, a dentist, a florist, a weekly newspaper, a funeral home, a nursery, a laundromat, a car wash, a feed mill, a farm chemicals dealer, a machinist, a welding repair shop, a cabinet maker, a tax preparer, and a veterinarian. As is true everywhere else, businesses come and go, and it is a continuing question of which ones will be able to survive in the long run.

Thorstein Veblen, in his classic description of small towns in 1923, observed that the central thrust of Main Street businesses is to seek monopoly status, driving out the competition. Today, the chief concern of small town businessmen is competition from outside discount stores, malls, mail order warehouses, E-commerce, and other sellers who divert local residents from shopping at home. In response, Clear Lake's Community Club works to promote a variety of community activities and, through them, to strengthen local businesses. It organizes parades and retail promotions like Crazy Days, assists with the annual Farm and Home Show, works to enhance the town's appearance, and holds an annual recognition banquet, honoring an employee and an employer of the year and giving out a community service award. Its biggest promotion, every August, is Hot Dog Days, when local merchants distribute free hot dogs (the number has risen from 100 in the early years to as many as 6000 lately) and other food items and also mark down merchandise as a way of thanking their customers for their patronage.

Clear Lake is typical of towns established in the northern Plains and Midwest when the railroad arrived during the late nineteenth century. During the first surge of optimism and entrepreneurial zeal, more stores and businesses emerged than towns could sustain, and the story over the years was one of a weeding-out process, in which the number of establishments fluctuated, as proprietors came and went. Eventually their numbers declined, until the problem was no longer that there were too many of them but that there were often none at all.

Clear Lake's population has remained relatively stable, hovering between 1,100 and 1,350 for the past half-century. That is attributable to Clear Lake's status as a county seat and to concerted efforts by town leaders. As the typical farm size has grown from a quarter section or two to two thousand acres or more, the population living in the country, which provides the customer base for businesses in town, has halved and then declined further. With birth rates and family size in retreat both on the farm and in town, the population of Clear Lake would have declined significantly had it not been for an influx of retired farmers and, more recently, the establishment of several factories, some of whose workers live in town and some of whom commute from other places.

Two major manufacturing concerns contribute substantially to the economic health of the community—Empi, which manufactures medical devices, and Tek Ord (Technical Ordinance, Inc.), which produces munitions components. Both employ between 150 and 170 workers. The Gopher Sign Company, Supreme Welding, and ITC (a telephone co-op and cable television distributor) provide jobs for between thirty and thirty-five people each. Many of their workers commute from other towns and rural areas, while an increasing number of people who live in Clear Lake drive to nearby towns like Brookings and Watertown to work in factories and other businesses.

Crucial in getting these companies to locate in Clear Lake was a Community Development Corporation that enlisted the volunteer services of numerous businessmen, professionals, and other community residents. On matters such as this, the willingness of individuals to contribute their time and, often, some financial assistance, and the belief that the community will benefit from such cooperative effort are crucial to success. Clear Lake sought and obtained recognition from state government as a GOLD community (the acronym standing for Guide to Opportunities for Local Development) after it had demonstrated efforts to improve its business climate and social amenities.

In addition, Clear Lake, like many towns its size, contains a reliable group of two or three dozen people whom residents can count on to take the lead on matters such as industrial development, school bond issues, governmental decisions, and other issues concerning the community as a whole. In these situations, the "80/20 Rule" generally operates. This is the idea that eighty percent of the work gets done by twenty percent of the people. Often, a smaller core of a half-dozen or so businessmen, professionals, and community leaders identify problems, define issues, establish priorities, and work to improve community involvement. Several civic-minded, strong-willed individuals can contribute greatly to a community's success in facing the kinds of challenges that inevitably arise. However, to succeed, a town requires not only dedicated leaders but also willing followers who will cooperate and contribute to the achievement of collective goals.

In recent years, it has become more difficult to obtain that kind of volunteer effort in Clear Lake, in part because of a decline in the number of people available to participate in such activities. During the fifties and sixties, the Community Club had sixty-five to seventy members who would gather in church basements for evening meals and meetings. Now they do well to have fifteen people at meetings. Since organizing itself with thirty charter members in 1956, the Kiwanis Club has experienced fluctuations in its membership; once up to forty, it currently numbers about half that. The Lions Club likewise has experienced a membership drop. It encourages participation by holding regular dinners that spouses also attend. Both organizations have opened up their membership to women, which has bolstered their participation rates. A snowmobile club is also active in town.

Organizations of all kinds generally have found it difficult to recruit members, officers, and volunteers to get the work done. The reason often given is that people are too busy to take on another time commitment or responsibility. With two-career families now the norm, people sometimes working two jobs, more time spent in commuting, and other pressures on their time, such explanations are persuasive. But Clear Lake has also been as much affected by the attractions of electronic entertainment as communities everywhere else, and obviously many people have traded more active involvement in neighborhood and community affairs for the electronic hearth of television, computers, and video games. As a result, many organizations struggle to maintain membership or merely to survive.

Extension clubs, which used to be quite active both in town and in the countryside, have likewise dwindled considerably. Boy and Girl Scout Troops, Cub Scouts and Brownies, and 4-H organizations continue to operate, but it is often difficult to keep them going. Ladies' aids remain strong in the Catholic and Lutheran churches, but have fallen off in the Baptist and Congregational churches.

One activity that remains popular, however, as is true almost everywhere, is high school athletics. Since girls' sports were given a boost by Title IX of federal education legislation in 1972, a whole new dimension has emerged. High school sporting events often bring out the largest crowds of any activity. Since going to town on Saturday night died out, school sporting events have become the main occasions for the entire community to mingle—young and old, male and female, different occupational and social groups, and a variety of ethnic and religious groups. Clear Lake's sports teams are sources of town pride, and sports news remains a major part of weekly coverage in the local newspaper. Booster Club activities bring out parents and provide opportunities for people to work together to advance school spirit and defray expenses. Much community involvement, both for those who have students in their families and for those who do not, revolves around the schools.

People in towns like Clear Lake cannot rely on others to do what needs to be done; they have to get involved themselves. In a variety of ways, active participation in community affairs is necessary for a town to thrive. A dramatic example of this kind of commitment was the fund-raising campaign for building an addition to the Clear Lake Hospital and Clinic. With one doctor, a doctor's assistant, and a visiting cardiologist in the community, town residents rely upon and take pride in their hospital and clinic. Keeping the hospital running has been difficult and has required considerable financial sacrifice. Controversy over policies and individual doctors has divided the community in the past. But most people recognize the advantages their facility confers and have willingly assisted in keeping it operating.

The Deuel County Memorial Hospital employs about eighty people and operates on an annual budget of $6.5 million. In 2000 and 2001, a major fund-raising campaign was conducted to raise $400,000 from community residents to go along with a bond issue, reserve funds, and money from Sioux Valley Hospitals & Health System for a $1.7 million facility expansion project. Other campaigns to raise funds for the hospital had been successfully conducted in the past. The plan for this drive was worked out with the assistance of a professional fundraiser, and a committee of approximately sixty local people fanned out through the community to solicit contributions. An eight-page brochure listed twenty-five specific designated gift opportunities, ranging from $3,000 apiece to $50,000. It mapped out a plan focusing special attention on large donors, hoping to attract one gift in the range of $75,000, another of $50,000, one of $25,000, three of $15,000, five of $10,000, and lesser amounts. Prospective donors were informed that their gifts would "contribute significantly to the economy of Clear Lake and Deuel County."

One prominent argument in the home visits was that maintaining a hospital in Clear Lake would boost property values. For example, to prevent an $80,000 house from losing $20,000 of its value, which might happen if the hospital shut down, it would make economic sense for a person to make a $5,000 or $10,000 contribution. The fund drive thus wedded personal pecuniary interest to community betterment. Ground was broken on the new facility in July, 2000, and by November the fund drive was 90 percent complete. When the open house celebration for the new facility was held a year after groundbreaking, the entire amount had been pledged. The fund drive raised approximately $300 per capita, an impressive indication of community support. In addition, three other highly visible evidences of the vitality of the community and the importance of volunteer efforts are the construction during the past several years of a new fire hall, a new community center, and a major addition to the school.

Generosity shows itself in a variety of other ways in Clear Lake. As was the case with the hospital fund drive, willingness to give reflects a combi-

nation of genuine altruism and self-interest. People feel a sense of obligation to help their neighbors and to better the community, but they also realize that they will benefit from the results, too. They know that they may
be the ones on the receiving end the next time. When someone gets hurt,
the town holds a benefit. Cub Scouts conduct an annual food drive, church
groups sponsor a continuous round of soup suppers, and fund-raisers of
all kinds are common—for the hospital, for a new floor in the gymna-
sium, for the Clear Lake restoration project (dredging the lake), and for
other programs. The Lions and Kiwanis clubs, the Scouts, 4-H, and
Booster Club all run their own fundraisers. "People are incredibly generous in these small towns," one newcomer said, "but I've never seen
giving like I've seen here."

The *Clear Lake Courier* frequently reports on these kinds of activities
in its columns, such as the Sharing Tree at Christmastime for needy
children, bake sales at the Good Samaritan Center, benefit basketball
games to raise money for medical expenses for families, the junior class's
magazine drive, the fire department's annual raffle, a talent night at the
Congregational church to raise money to send students to a national
conference, a holiday breakfast and bazaar for the Wellness Center, the
New Hope Walk for Cancer, periodic appearances of the Red Cross Blood-
mobile, Lions Club candy sales, sale of the Kiwanis Club's calendar, and
the Cancer Golf Tournament.

When asked how they think about their town, Clear Lake residents
offer a variety of words to describe it. "Conservative" is one term frequently
mentioned. "Conservative morally, ethically, fiscally," says one resident.
"People are very independent." But while residents try to be self-sufficient,
one of the things that makes the town livable is the belief that other people will help out in a pinch. Religion remains important in most people's
lives, and Clear Lake is a town of churches: St. Paul's Lutheran (ELCA);
Trinity Evangelical Lutheran (WELS); St. Mary's Catholic; United Methodist; First Baptist; and First Congregational (UCC). Churches here face
the same kinds of pressures drawing people away from them as elsewhere,
but the churches of Clear Lake retain a strong hold on people's lives.
Germans, Norwegians, and Scandinavians in general retain a dispropor-

tionate presence in the population, which, one resident noted, is "very white." Blacks and other ethnic minorities are notable by their almost complete absence, a situation that is taken for granted by most of the population but which strikes outsiders with considerable force. Intergenerational links are more tenuous than they were in the fifties or even twenty years ago. The youth culture engulfs students here as everywhere else, but there are probably more contacts between the generations in Clear Lake than in many places in the United States. That can be seen especially in a program at the high school that links students and elderly residents whom the young people visit regularly in their homes.

However, a newcomer to the community observed: "It is hard for an outsider to feel welcome in this town." No doubt there are others who feel the same way. Still, most Clear Lake residents do not consider themselves to be standoffish or cliquish. Every morning, a dozen or so men gather at 8 a.m. at the Lunch Box Café on the east side of Main Street for coffee. (Other coffee groups meet as early as 5:30 a.m. at the Cowboy gas station, Melvee's Bar, and Kathy's Corner Café.) Some of the regulars also have a little breakfast. They get out the dice and shake three or four times to see who's going to pay for coffee and toast. For an outsider, breaking into a group like this might seem difficult, but the men do not think of themselves as exclusive. One woman I talked to discovered people in town to be friendly, but she took the initiative to establish contact with them. She obtained the name of someone who liked to play golf, called her on the phone, and asked if she could join her for a round. The difference between people who find the town cliquish and those who remark on its friendliness often lies in how willing the newcomers are to make advances. Besides meeting and getting to know one's neighbors, associating with people at work and meeting them at church remain some of the best ways for newcomers to get acquainted.

The town also seems to be suffering confusion over its identity. On the one hand, some people are intent on building it up economically and maintaining primacy of place in the area. Others are more willing to go with the flow and accommodate themselves to economic realities. If Clear Lake is increasingly becoming a bedroom community for workers who drive to Brookings and Watertown, many people don't see anything wrong with that. It's twenty minutes to Watertown, thirty to Brookings. People will cope one way or another, they believe, and the important thing is to maintain a sense of togetherness and helpfulness, whatever the economic fortunes of the town.

One of the major attractions of Clear Lake and other small towns like it is the relatively cheap housing. Older houses, especially, can be had for thousands of dollars less than in larger urban places. The slower, quieter lifestyle appeals to many people, and residents are quick to note that your neighbors know and look out for you here.

Actually, the assurance that your neighbors know who you are and will come to your aid in an emergency is an expectation that becomes less certain as time goes by. In small towns such as Clear Lake, as a larger share of the population commutes to other places to work, it is not always so certain that you will be acquainted with or even know who your neighbors are. While community-mindedness remains stronger here than in many places in America, time pressures and the withering away of traditional rituals and practices attenuate those ties. No longer do Memorial Day ceremonies draw out most of the community. Other holidays remain important, but families tend to go their own ways in celebrating them. Ball games bring excitement to the community, but not like they did in the past. Only a few times a year, such as homecoming time, Hot Dog Days, and the annual rodeo, is there anything like the community presence on Main Street that commonly used to occur on Saturday nights.

That is why groups like Emergency Medical Technicians and the Fire Department, both staffed completely by volunteers, stand out so impressively for their volunteer spirit. The Ambulance Service relies upon thirty EMTs—divided evenly between men and women—who go through 120 hours of training to qualify for their positions. Being on call three or four days at a time, with seven days off in between, they have to be ready for all kinds of medical emergencies, from car wrecks to heart attacks. The washout rate during training is fifty percent. Some people are not prepared for the sight of blood; others aren't ready to sacrifice their freedom to so rigorous a schedule. The unit responds to about 160 calls a year. They have received as many as six calls on a single day. Then they may go for a week or ten days without any calls.

The EMTs work hand in glove with the fire department, whose only paid member is the chief, who receives several hundred dollars a year for organizing and managing his volunteer crew. Much of the appeal of the fire department is the camaraderie among the twenty-six men who compose it. They spend one night a month training and brushing up on procedures, another night working on equipment. Once a year they organize a raffle to help pay for equipment and supplies. Without the many hours of volunteer labor supplied by both of these groups, Clear Lake residents would have to pony up a considerable amount of cash to pay for fire protection and emergency assistance.

In thinking about the many aspects of community that remain pervasive in Clear Lake, it is obvious that the quality of life in the town depends heavily upon the assets, talents, and actions that people contribute without being paid for it. People look out for each other, in part, because they expect that they will be helped when they need it. Such reciprocal relationship trades on people's notion of fairness and mutual obligation. Many people help others, however, simply out of altruism, which is often connected to religious attitudes and beliefs. They assist others not out of expectation of compensation, but because they want to do it and like to do it.

While problem-solving requires work and effort, much of what makes a community pleasurable and desirable is the opportunity to simply enjoy one's neighbors and fellow townspeople. If anybody doubts the vitality of community in Clear Lake, let that person go to the Lanes Bowling Center. Begun enthusiastically in 1940, bowling leagues remain a vital presence in town. There are so many leagues tying up the eight alleys on most evenings that there isn't much time left for open bowling. Friday and Saturday nights are the best times for non-league bowlers. In Clear Lake, at least, the phenomenon of "bowling alone" is not much in evidence.

The future of towns like Clear Lake will remain heavily dependent upon population developments, job opportunities, economic trends, government actions, and other factors that make it possible for people to survive financially. But what holds many people here is the strong sense of community, which compensates for a certain amount of economic deprivation. People crave social interaction, even as they also desire to preserve their freedom and expand their opportunities. Many are willing to sacrifice some material benefit for the close personal ties that still constitute the core of community in many small towns. This sense of community is what makes life livable for many people. Those hoping to enhance the quality of community life will do well to look at the example of towns like Clear Lake.

People in Clear Lake know that it takes effort, cooperation, a willingness to work, personal sacrifice, and generosity for a community to achieve its full potential. Leadership is essential, but followers are also needed and a willingness on the part of the larger group to work together. Finally, there is the matter of organization. Individual effort and personal ingenuity can go a long way, but communities like Clear Lake work best where institutions function effectively, providing a firm foundation for generating the social capital that enables them to survive and succeed.

A Note on Sources

The information in this article was obtained primarily from articles in the local weekly newspaper, the *Clear Lake Courier*, and from interviews with Clear Lake residents. For these, I would especially like to thank Joyce Cook, Gary DeJong, Gordon Engen, Blaine Franken, Yvonne Gauger, Darrell Halse, Michael Haug, Gerry Koenecke, Gerry Law, Mark Law, Robert Law, Clint Miller, and Jon Puetz. The Clear Lake Commercial Club and the City Government office kindly provided statistics and information. I would also like to thank Mike Lauritsen, team leader for the Community Resource Team that visited Clear Lake on November 14-16, 2006, to do a community assessment under the auspices of the South Dakota Rural Development Council. Their listening sessions provided updates for much of the information in the essay, as did the opportunity to go on a tour of the town with them. Obviously, I take responsibility for all statements in the essay and any mistakes contained therein.

Discussion Questions:

1. Compare the sense of community in Clear Lake (and in your own town) with what it was in earlier decades.

2. What forces are working to build up community and to tear it down?

3. Does your town have an identifiable core of leaders who generally take the lead in promoting community interests?

4. Does the "80-20 Rule" operate in your town? How can leaders work to get everyone involved in promoting community?

5. Has your town recently gotten involved in a project similar to Clear Lake's $400,000 fund-raising drive for its hospital and clinic? If so, describe it.

6. Why is it becoming more difficult to promote community betterment? Or is it? What do you think can be done to help solicit more volunteer effort?

Dakota Town

for David Allan Evans

Doug Cockrell

The elevator stands watchman,
its windows claimed
by the stones hurled by
boys who have left.
Now there are tires moaning
over the highways bringing
wind gusts past the last gas pump
where an old man in overalls watches
headlights and taillights
all day.

The streets are just Dakota summer dust
where the rain sinks untouched
to the sewers that have stopped their
hissings through the pipes,
and the outhouses are filled to the brim.

A farmer has jerked his country school
from its roots among the uncut weeds
and his haystack mover has taken it
to his home outside the town.

The church, the bar,
the hardware store and the lumberyard
have been claimed
for fences and windbreaks.

The graveyard lies at the edge
of a cornfield by the edge of town,
along the highway ditch,
the tombstones among sunflowers nodding
at the moaning tires going by.

Discussion Questions:

1. Which images and image pairings in this poem are most expressive?

2. Could a community like the one described in this poem be restored?
   If so, how? If not, why not?

The Lucky B

Darla Bielfeldt

The "B" in The Lucky B was for Bliss, as in its owner, Phyllis Bliss, and not happiness.

Phyllis was, in fact, perhaps one of the most unhappy, retracted, gray people I have ever met. She and her husband, Charlie, were scrawny, practically living on coffee and cigarettes, but their dogs ate well. Each night they would take home gallon-sized tin cans of food left behind by the people who came in and left the tiny restaurant in my hometown.

Every day after high school I would walk, carrying my navy and red plaid uniform, two straight blocks to The Lucky B. After changing in the restroom, I would fill a plastic ice cream bucket with soapy water, throw a hard, green sponge in to soak, and take it all outside to wash the Lunch Special from the front window. Actually, it wasn't the Special itself—our customers, although not genteel, did refrain from throwing food; rather, I removed a listing of the Special. Then, with white shoe polish, I would write the Evening Special across the entire window: Chicken Fried Steak or Chicken Strips or, on special occasions, Rocky Mountain Oysters.

Passing cars would stop in the middle of Main Street long enough for me to finish the letter that would trigger recognition. Usually some old man would lean out his window and holler, "What's on?" or, if he felt frisky, "What's cookin', Good Lookin'?" Most days I was pleased for the chance to stand outside the greasy restaurant and for the possibility of being honked at by a Ford-ful of guys, but when I had to write the special Special, I felt oddly ashamed. I may as well have written Bull Balls: Hot & Crunchy! Get 'em hot! Get 'em fresh!

To our customers, "Special" did not mean "Gourmet," but a guarantee for leftovers tomorrow. They needed strength more than the palatal experiences, quantity more than quality. We had a reputation for giving huge amounts of food on the special plates, and in a community where getting your money's worth was highly—and necessarily—valued, appearing generous was just plain good business.

Our cook prided himself on the portions. He was a man of overflowing abundance who looked like an ex-con-but-Jesus-loving boy. I never believe he was a licensed chef, even though he said so and wore a white paper hat as proof. Somehow, however, this man, who started sausage gravy by melting a pound of old French fry grease, had acquired a large beautiful cookbook. It may have been the prettiest thing in The Lucky B. He would show it to me during slow times, his hands nearly trembling as he turned the pages to a glossy picture of a chocolate dessert: "I make this," he would declare softly, as if reminding himself of who he was at his center.

"Yes, yes," would come the faithful response of his wife who served him as prep cook. "It's rich. Twelve layers there, you see, then all that sauce on top."

The cookbook may have been beautiful, but they were the homeliest couple I have ever seen. She and the cook had been married when she was just thirteen; they were strangers in town and rumored Mormons. The wife's hair was thin and receding, and she wore it in a long greasy ponytail, the ragged end groping down the middle of her wide back. Her smile was also wide, but her eyes were small and close, dark like raisins. She was, to put it bluntly, gut-wrenchingly ugly in a way which until I got to know her, made it difficult for me to look at her directly. Despite this, however, I did not pity her because she was kind, and even back then I had a small understanding of how kindness and generosity create their own beauty. The café's regular customers didn't all receive kindness from me. Most of them were the sons of poor men who gathered every afternoon to drink coffee and talk about farming. They seemed extremely concerned with increasing bushel per acre and controlling weeds—to keep them as tame as their imaginations, I suspected. I thought it was ironic that in order to gain sympathy about how their hard work went unappreciated, they sat in The Lucky B for hours. Pulling the tables together, and sometimes using all twenty chairs, they would form a grumbling community.

I never knew their names, but devised my own system to keep their orders straight by determining the angle and direction at which each man's seed company cap sat on his head: Ham and eggs over to 45' Right; biscuits and gravy to Over Left Eye; short stack to Way Back. It proved effective. When they made rude comments or stared I would fill their cups until the coffee was hanging over the edge and pray it would scald their fingers on the next drink. Generosity? No.

I did learn one of the men's names out of dislike for the others. He was an older man, a washed-up, boozed-up cowboy, and they scornfully called him Runt. He had probably been called similar things all his life, so in my own mean way of spiting the other men, I decided to call him by his given name. It was Earl and I would sweetly fling it at the men when I could: "Here you go, Earl. Want some more coffee, Earl." Kindness? No, just my way of judging the others' faults, pointing out our difference, setting myself above.

Unfortunately, Earl was a trusting soul, and believed I was simply being kind to him. He adored me for this and wanted to repay me. After a few hours of talking, he would rise from the rest and start his painful shuffle to where I stood behind the cash register. It seriously took him three or four minutes to walk across the seven feet of red carpet and my abhorrence grew with every second. I had ample time to see the weariness of his eyes, the brown film of dried tobacco juice around his mouth and down his chin, the urine stains on his left pant leg.

When he reached me he would smile shyly, then slowly and deeply press a dime, always a dime, into the palm of my hand. The men at the table would nudge one another and wink at the cook, who stood watching through his little window framed with tiny bags of potato chips.

The dime would be sticky, and there was never a time when I didn't throw Runt's gift into the trash, never a time I didn't make sure the other men saw me do it. I wanted them to see. I would wait until Runt was nearly out the door, and then, with a look of exaggerated disgust, would pry the coin from my palm and let it plop into the wastebasket behind my counter. I suppose I wanted the others to know by my mean act that I was one of them, still on my way out, and don't you forget it, but not out yet.

Some days I feel more ashamed of these small mean acts—the coffee, the dimes—than I feel about most things I've done in life. None of it was pure. It was all designed to separate and divide, but now, nearly 25 years away from The Lucky B, it's much too late to find my way back home to make amends. There's no apologizing for my unkindness, for the ways I held myself above the people I knew at The Lucky B.

The café closed long ago. The cook, owner, and most of the men who sat drinking coffee every afternoon are dead. I wish I could say I learned my lesson well—that now I truly appreciate everyone I meet, grateful for their generosity and the simple gifts they bring—but accepting and giving kindness and generosity takes a courage I'm still mustering up.

Earl, I'm sure, is long buried on the hill a mile north of town, although I don't remember hearing the news. There would be no reason to know I would care. No reason to believe it would matter now that I'm this far away from home.

Discussion Questions:

1. What might this essay suggest about relationships between generations in community life?

2. What does the term "grumbling community" mean to you? How might this term apply to most, or even all, communities?

3. How might you define "beauty" and "ugliness"? Can you find examples of both in this essay?

4. Why does the author refer to Earl as "Runt" in describing her disdain for him, and then use his real name again at the end of the essay?

5. What concerns are expressed by the author in the conclusion of the essay? Do you share her concerns?

6. How might the experiences the author has described in this essay affect the rest of her life?

Town Team

William Kloefkorn

The local jocks back home in Attica
seem more than amply snugged.

At first base a stomach extends itself
to scoop a low throw, like a gunslug,
from the dust.

The shortstop moves like a sweet fat fairy
to his right or left,
his sneakers leaking ballbearings

Outfielders jog for several days to their positions,
pivot like bloated ballerinas,
doff their caps,
then jog for several days back to the dugout.

The infield is a squat and pussel-gutted chain.
round faced and red, it
chews its tongue and
spits practically perfest daisies.

The pitcher trembles the mound with a headshake:
he wants another sign.
The catcher, wide as a sandcrab,
sweats marbles.

At the plate
a batter settles into his stance
like a tender, untapped keg.

Discussion Questions::

1. Why is baseball sometimes referred to as "America's game?" What does it represent, in towns large and small? How might it create and maintain community?

2. What are some other activities that create and maintain community, in your experience?

3. What kind of community is represented in this poem?

Citizen Participation in the Councils of Government: A Defense Against County Consolidation

Delmer Lonowski

Local governments in South Dakota, like those in many other states, face a dilemma. Citizens are demanding lower taxes while at the same time demanding the same or higher levels of government services. Proposals for county consolidation have been introduced into the legislature based on the belief that consolidation will result in more efficient and effective local government and that economies of scale will be obtained. However, consolidation is very difficult to achieve because people are reluctant to give up their local courthouses and local control over the things that directly affect their lives.

Local governments are markedly independent, separated geographically, with little interaction among them. Citizens identify with their local governments because they know each other and local government decision-makers whom they control and from whom they receive benefits. Local identity often translates into feelings similar to nationalism, leading to competition with other local governments for scarce resources and population. However, cooperation among local governments is possible when there is mutual need, and especially when there is an economic incentive.

Councils of governments (COG) are regional organizations that institutionalize such cooperation, making possible additional local government services otherwise not available, because of a lack of resources.

COGs help overcome this lack because the member governments share the costs of such services (ACIR, 1973: 259). South Dakota has six COGs that can be vehicles for achieving the benefits of consolidation while preserving and maintaining local control.

According to the Advisory Commission on Intergovernmental Relations (1973: 51), a COG is "a multi-functional voluntary regional association of elected local officials or local governments organized to promote common interests without member units subordinating any of their powers to the body." COGs are not governmental units. They lack governmental powers and operating responsibilities such as taxing power and the right to exercise eminent domain. They are usually limited to planning, promoting dialogue, providing technical assistance and facilitating joint purchasing.

COGs promote common interests by bringing local governments together to discuss common local and regional problems. In doing so, they facilitate joint cooperation and planning to solve such social and physical problems as crime and the need to provide road maintenance. With the development of expertise in COG staffs, the COGs can lobby both state and federal governments on behalf of their member local governments (Wikstrom, 1977: 81-99).

Presently, local governments in South Dakota and elsewhere are threatened both because of economic constraints and because of the questioning of local governmental structures. Some believe that there are too many local governments duplicating too many services, and that local governments would be more economical if consolidated into larger regional governments.

State government can force consolidation. However, such action eliminates local participation in decisions, which is necessary for local cooperation. Local participation gives the people a sense of ownership. In addition, state action tends to create one-size-fits-all forms of regional governance. Opposition to consolidation schemes stems from local people wanting to preserve their community identities and to preserve local control over government decisions that affect their lives. COGs can both bring about the desired economies and maintain local control.

In a series of articles, Allan Wallis (1994a, b, c) describes COGs as constituting waves of development. In his final article, he suggests that to move into the final wave, COGs need to develop both management capacity and legitimacy. He argues that to the extent that COGs are perceived to be legitimate, they will be given the capacity to develop and carry out decisions. He sets forth a two-phase plan to achieve legitimacy: 1. create a vision of the region's future; and 2. institutionalize or structure a mechanism to generate that vision. He argues that the vision which will be created will provide the legitimacy the governing mechanisms need (Wallis, 1994a: 448-451).

William Dodge (1992) makes a similar argument, noting that we need a third model located between, on the one hand, autonomous local governments occasionally cooperating with each other and on the other, regional governments. Dodge suggests a mechanism which he calls SIGNET—Strategic Intercommunity Governance Networks, working to solve local problems, placing emphasis on the contributions of the entire community: public, private, academic, nonprofit, foundation, civic organizations and individual citizens. He believes that these organizations and individuals combined possess capabilities and capacities necessary to generate new visions and to deliver intercommunity services (Dodge, 1992: 408-412).

A fundamental requirement in both Wallis's (1994a) Two-Phases and Dodge's (1992) SIGNET is to increase citizen participation in the activities of the COGs. Many COGs are already taking steps in this direction by organizing citizen advisory committees and task forces which provide citizen participation in the planning processes or to support COG initiatives (Henderson, 1990: 109). However, these committees and task forces require expending considerable COG resources to organize.

Wallis (1994a: 307-308) suggests that the networks should be based on the already existing regional civic infrastructures, including all organizations, public, private, and nonprofit (local governments, universities, chambers of commerce, civic clubs). These organizations can work together because of shared norms and trust at the local level. Each possesses organizational capacities. Acting alone, they cannot solve a specific problem; however, acting cooperatively, they may have the capacity to address a region's problems. Wallis suggests that COGs are the most effective conveners of this network relationship. However, if these organizations are to play a role, he believes, they must be accorded representation on the COGs (Wallis, 1994a: 460).

The key for South Dakota COG development seems to lie with the COGs themselves. Any visions for addressing the needs of a region and the capacity to address those needs must be generated by the people of the region. The COGs possess the ability to bring the people together to generate such visions. If COGS are going to defend their counties against consolidation, they need to increase the capacities and efficiencies of their local governments. This cannot be achieved simply by providing services to local governments. To achieve those visions, local government activities need to be coordinated to provide better services more efficiently. COGs cannot now provide this coordination because they lack legitimacy. The representatives on COG boards are representatives of local governments and consequently, only indirectly represent the people of the region. However, if private and non-profit organizations were provided representation on COG boards, the boards would be more representative and hence, more legitimate. Citizens participating through these organizations would provide COGs with the support and resources necessary to bring about the coordination of local government activities.

South Dakota's counties face the threat that if they do not take action to improve service and efficiency, the state may consolidate them, thereby reducing local control. However, the state faces the possible problem outlined by Kadlecek (1997): voters repeatedly rejecting merger plans because they prefer local autonomy. Expanding citizen participation in COG decision-making can both increase the legitimacy of COGs and local government capacities and satisfy the preferences for local autonomy.

In South Dakota, the impetus for the creation of COGs came out of the governor's office. In 1970, Governor Frank Farrar proposed the creation of South Dakota's COGs because the state's local governments were not equal to the tasks implied by the Nixon Administration's "New Federalism." South Dakota's COGs were organized through the enabling legislation of the Joint Powers Act and after Governor Farrar designated district boundaries by executive order. Governor Farrar divided the state into six districts. South Dakota's COGs are self-described as flexible, accountable, and efficient "grassroots" associations that have demonstrated their usefulness to private and nonprofit business and local, state, and federal agencies (Profile, 1994: 1-2).

South Dakota's COGs are engaged in grant and application writing, organizing project packages that involve multiple funding sources, project development and the administration of the grants once received. Most of this activity is for business and economic development and for securing funding for local government infrastructure. In support of these primary objectives, the COGs engage in planning and zoning assistance, environmental planning and research and education. They are involved in ordinance development and revision, particularly in zoning. COGs have also developed expertise in water quality research and rural water system management. Their most recent activity is in the development of Geographic Information Systems (GIS) using the Global Positioning System (GPS). The COGs' role in the development of many state and local programs will be greatly enhanced by the data obtained from these systems.

The state is beginning to make more use of COGs, as COGs are providing contract services for state agencies, particularly the Department of Environment and Natural Resources and the Department of Transportation. The COGs possess much of the data that these departments need in their decisions. This will become increasingly important when GIS/GPS is fully developed, because the COGs will possess more of the information that these decision-makers will require.

Former Governor William Janklow made significant use of COGs. The Governor's Office of Economic Development placed a representative in three of the COGs' offices. These representatives were assigned to work with the business communities in the respective regions, providing business development counseling. Janklow also relied on COGs to administer his Senior Housing Program, which puts inmates to work constructing housing for senior citizens.

South Dakota's COGs follow the pattern of COGs around the country. To examine the potential for movement into either Wallis's (1994a) Two-Phase model or Dodge's (1992) SIGNET, South Dakota's six COGs will be considered individually.

The First District Association of Local Governments is comprised of the eleven counties located in the east-central part of the state.[1] The First District's board consists of a county commissioner from each county, a municipal office holder recruited from the largest community in each county, and a citizen chosen by county and municipal representatives. The chair of the Santee Sioux Tribe is also a member of the board.

Most of the First District's funding comes from dues (a per capita charge for each county), fees, and grant administration. Its major activity has been in planning and zoning, particularly as pertaining to livestock confinement regulations, resulting in a subtle form of cooperation. The ordinances developed by the First District staff are quite similar, which is partially due to the same staff person or people writing the ordinances. This makes it difficult for confinement operators to escape regulation by simply moving into the next county. The District encourages cooperation wherever possible among its member governments, but most intergovernmental cooperation develops on its own as counties and municipalities see a need.

The six counties that comprise the South Eastern Council of Governments (SECOG) are located in the southeast corner of the state.[2] This council is the closest example that South Dakota has to a traditional urban council. It is predominantly urban, as it includes Sioux Falls and the rapidly growing corridor along Interstate 29 that leads to Sioux City, Iowa. Consequently, SECOG's primary objective is managing the expansion and development of the regional economy while ensuring that adequate infrastructure exists to accommodate this growth.

While SECOG has the smallest board, it is unique in that it includes members of the state legislature. The SECOG board has one representative from each county, three representatives from Sioux Falls, one from Vermillion, and one small town representative from each of the six counties. Four members of the state legislature from the region are named by the member-county boards to the SECOG board. Board members are typically office holders, although ordinary citizens can be appointed. Citizens are involved in various projects, but much depends on the extent that the county boards want to involve citizens.

A major weakness is that many of SECOG's activities involve crisis management, with little real planning. Most are in reaction to the tremendous economic growth that is occurring between Sioux Falls and North Sioux City. A second weakness is that SECOG is heavily dependent on outside funding, deriving approximately 66% of its income from federal or state programs. Any cutbacks at these two levels could be devastating to SECOG.

At the same time, SECOG has achieved high levels of intergovernmental cooperation. It facilitated a dialogue among juvenile agencies to ensure that their activities did not overlap. This led to the identification of a need for a juvenile facility, a facility that was beyond the means of the member governments individually and perhaps even of the region. SECOG worked out arrangements with its members and other counties beyond the region to establish a fourteen-county facility. It presently is working on developing a telecommunication judicial service that will make possible court appearances via telecommunications technology to reduce the cost of transporting prisoners.

Planning and Development District III consists of fifteen counties situated in the south-central part of the state.[3] It has a sixty-person board of directors. The board has one representative from each county and one from each municipality with a population of 100. The Yankton and Lower Brule Tribes are also represented. Twenty percent of the board must consist of citizens who do not hold elective office. There is no formal procedure to obtain this 20 percent. If the board is not properly constituted, some elected officials are replaced with lay citizens. An interesting aspect of this board is that a variety of quasi-governmental agencies, such as water development districts, resource conservation and development districts, and landfill associations, are also represented. Only the counties and municipalities with populations more than 500 have a vote. All other entities have a voice but not a vote in the decision-making process. This is not critical, as the board decides most issues on consensus.

The district emphasizes cooperation to achieve its goals. The district runs the housing and tourism programs for its members. It is represented in the Missouri Valley Health Care Network, making local health care a cooperative arrangement. The executive director feels that there is a potential for cooperation amongst District III's school districts. He sees much duplication of effort and a failure to accomplish objectives because of the lack of school district resources.

The Northeast Council of Governments (NECOG) includes the thirteen counties and one hundred communities in the northeast part of the state.[4] The fifty-four member board has four representatives from each county: two county commissioners, the mayor of the largest community, and a citizen chosen by the county board. Brown County, the most populous county, receives one extra representative, the mayor of Groton. The Sisseton-Wahpeton Sioux Tribe is also represented. One-third of the board members are citizens who do not hold elective office.

NECOG has a close working relationship with the private sector on many of its projects and programs. Many of NECOG's projects and programs are citizen-driven. An example of this close working relationship with the private sector is the development of an internet connection for the area. The region was initially left out of internet development because private enterprise did not feel that it was worthwhile, owing to the small population in the area. NECOG coordinated fifteen public and private partners, including local governments, power companies, schools and others, to obtain an internet connection. The group obtained funding from a variety of sources, purchased technology and trained people in its uses.

The Central South Dakota Enhancement District is a newly-reorganized COG that encompasses six counties.[5] It is a sparsely-populated region that includes only one major town, the state capitol, Pierre. Even Pierre is a small town, with only 13,000 people. About one-third of its workforce is employed in government. The district was reorganized in 2000 after more than twenty years without any regional organization. This COG is attempting to use a comprehensive economic development strategy by developing the region's economic resources and public facilities, by resource management, and by providing assistance to local service providers.

The Central South Dakota Board of Directors includes representatives of all dues-paying counties, municipalities and tribal governments. This membership currently includes six counties and ten municipalities. As a new COG, it has not yet acquired all of its potential members. The structure of this district approaches the two models discussed above. It provides for a committee of the general membership, which includes the representatives on the Board of Directors, and the possibility for representation from each school district and any local or regional organizations with an interest in rural development.

The Black Hills Council of Governments consists of eight counties located in the western one-fourth of the state.[6] Its political cultural characteristics, first identified by Daniel Elazar (1966), best explain its development. Unlike the other COGs, this region possesses what Elazar calls an "individualist" political culture. The expectation of its citizens is that government will stay out of their lives unless they ask it to intervene. The Black Hills Council adapts to this culture. It only responds to requests by its local governments. It is not deeply involved in developing cooperative arrangements within its region, confining itself only to servicing the needs of its members. From a financial perspective, one might argue that it is the strongest COG, because all but 16% of its income is self-generated, giving it a great deal of autonomy vis a vis the state and federal governments.

The Black Hills Council has twenty-three board members, representing counties and municipalities with populations of more than a thousand. Population differences are accommodated, with Rapid City having five members and Pennington County two. The communities with populations of more than a thousand are Hot Springs, Spearfish, and Lead. At one point, some smaller towns wanted seats, but lost interest when they found that they could receive all of the services of the COG without seats, since their counties were members. The Black Hills Council requires that ordinary citizens make up 20 percent of the council. The executive director likes to think of his council as consisting only of regular citizens because all of the elected officials are only part-time officials. A citizen advisory group is active on water issues.

The only real cooperation among the governments in the region is in the organization and operation of the Black Hills Council itself. Through the Council, these governments participate in the West Dakota Water Development District, the West River Coalition for Economic Development, and the Small Business Development Center. These activities are contact points with the citizenry as well. One other example of cooperation has resulted from the existence of the Black Hills Council, although this occurred outside the Council. This is in the organization of the Northern Hills Mayors' Association, which is involved in developmental cooperation and coordination. While the Association is not part of the Black Hills Council structure, it came into being because of the networking that occurred in the Council.

The most significant accomplishment of the Black Hills Council occurred when it acted as an interest group representing its member governments. The Black Hills Council successfully lobbied the state to pass the Energy Minerals Severance Tax that has yielded more than $10 million to member governments. It also challenged the U.S. Department of Interior's method of calculating payments to local governments from non-taxable federal lands. The Council's efforts obtained approximately $14 million for its member governments from the federal government (Black Hills Council, 1997). This seems to have been made possible by the autonomy identified above.

As shown above, COGs are a means to obtain goods and services which local governments acting alone cannot provide. Current arguments for consolidation are the same arguments made for COGs thirty years ago. However, at that time, COGs were often seen as the first step toward consolidation. Local governments resisted COG formation for the same reasons that they oppose county consolidation today. They did not want to lose local control (ACIR, 1973:115). However, the experience of thirty years has shown that COGs are not the first step toward consolidation. Most importantly, local governments control their COGs, preventing any movement toward consolidation when it is not in the interest of the local governments. Through the COGs, local governments obtain some benefits of consolidation without sacrificing local control. Unfortunately, the full potential of COGs has not been realized. South Dakota local governments are still faced with high costs and in some areas less than adequate services, leading to the continued consideration of county consolidation.

If local governments are going to defend themselves against the threat of consolidation, they need to develop the intergovernmental cooperation potential of their COGs. If the state is going to obtain the reductions in cost and the efficiencies promised by consolidation without the political costs, it needs to give local governments incentives to develop their COGs. The solutions suggested in the literature are Dodge's (1992) SIGNET and Wallis's (1994a) "Two-Phases." The main question is how to carry out such solutions. Part of the problem is lack of leadership. Local leaders exist, but they lack incentives to bring about COG development. The most obvious leaders are the COG executive directors. They, however, are accountable to their member-governments, who are primarily concerned with keeping the costs of government down. COGs are reluctant to attempt any projects that will not reduce the cost of government. They cannot take risks without reliable funding sources. Consequently, the executive directors are usually satisfied with the status quo and are unwilling to look at further development. The executive directors' main concerns are simply maintaining their organizations.

A second potential source of leadership can be found in the local governments. Each has elected leaders. It is possible that one of them in each region could become a regional leader. However, this is unlikely, because these leaders are primarily accountable only to their local voters. They have difficulty thinking and acting regionally. Some of these local leaders even serve on the COG boards. However, going back to their own city councils and county boards to sell the ideas generated in the COGs is difficult. Their colleagues on their councils and boards are even further removed from regional thinking. Added to this is the problem of frequent turnover of office holders on county boards and city councils, resulting in a need to educate the new members as to the possibilities that COGs represent.

Even if leadership could be found either in an executive director or in a local elected official, that person would only provide leadership to one

COG, to one region. This could lead to the development of a particular COG but would not solve the consolidation problem statewide. Therefore, leadership must come from the state level.

Three sources for leadership exist at the state level: state agencies, the legislature and the governor. State agencies can both facilitate COG development and state administrative efficiency by drawing state bureaucratic administrative boundaries to coincide with COG boundaries. They can arrange to provide technical support to the COGs. They can establish direct communication links so that COGs can affect bureaucratic decision-making. One problem with this approach, however, is that the state's bureaucratic agencies are divided into various functional areas. Their primary concerns are with their individual functions and not with the performance of the entire state system. Furthermore, they may be reluctant to give up some of their control to the COGs.

The state legislature could be a source of leadership. Unfortunately, however, most state legislators are as parochial as the political leaders found at the local level. They are concerned with problems in their own legislative districts, but no legislative district encompasses a region as large as any of the state's COG districts. In addition, in a state like South Dakota, where the legislature meets only a few weeks each year, it is not likely that an initiative will originate in the legislature without leadership from the governor or without significant grassroots support. However, the legislature does have a role here that will be described below.

This leaves us with the governor as the main source of leadership. The Janklow Administration provided us some examples of what the governor can do to further develop the state's COGs. Under Janklow, the state utilized the COGs to administer the Governor's Housing Program. It placed representatives of the Governor's Office of Economic Development in COG offices, enhancing communication between the state and the COGs. The administration used COG information and research capacities in developing state policy. There are other possibilities. The governor's office, through its control of the state bureaucracy, could also provide the incentives for the further development of COGs. For example, as it did in the case of the Governor's Housing Program, it could provide for the administration of state programs through COGs. The state could also require local government participation in COGs to obtain state services.

The problem with these suggestions is that they rely on a commitment from the governor for COG development. Finding a governor willing to make such a commitment may be possible, but there is no guarantee that the following governor will do similarly. The bureaucratic and administrative changes suggested must be institutionalized, and that will require legislative action (ACIR, 1973: 229). The problem of obtaining legislative support for such policies and programs can be overcome by the mechanism developed by SECOG. It is an excellent idea to have some members of the state legislature on each COG board. Not only does the COG then gain support in the legislature, but also individual legislators then gain an understanding of the problems faced by the COGs and member local governments. If all of the COGs were to follow this practice, the board-member legislators would compose 20-25% of the state legislature.

However, state level leadership would cause the same opposition to emerge as that faced by the county consolidation proposal. Local people would view the reforms as "top down" and threats to local autonomy. This problem can only be overcome with popular support for COG development. That support must be generated at the local level. David Berman (1993: 222) suggests that the continued development of COGs will require large-scale efforts to increase citizen participation in the COGs. This is where the two models discussed above become relevant to South Dakota. Nationally, many COGs are already expanding citizen participation through task forces and advisory committees. Task forces are ad hoc arrangements that involve citizens in finding solutions to particular problems. Advisory committees are permanent committees, usually composed of citizens and elected officials and staffed by COG professionals (Henderson, 1990: 109-110). Such structures do increase citizen participation, but this is not what Berman means by large scale efforts.

In both of the suggested models, visions for directions to take are developed by more than just the COG or just the region's local governments. Both models call for large-scale citizen involvement, developed through what Wallis calls a "coalition of interests" and what Dodge calls an "intercommunity governance network." Involving all of a region's interests in this governing network would give the COGs' visions legitimacy. It would also provide the local government representatives on the COG boards the support needed when they take COG decisions back to their local governments for action. It would provide the political support needed by the governor and the legislature to expand the role of South Dakota's COGs. It might also generate demands by the people of South Dakota that the governor and legislature act to make local government more efficient and effective.

To accomplish this, it seems essential that local interest groups have seats on the COG boards. Representation on COG boards would give these groups some ownership in the success of their COGs and their regions. There are two examples of such representation opportunity in South Dakota. Central South Dakota is willing to provide representation to all public or private organizations interested in economic development on its Committee of the General Membership. District III includes the various quasi-governmental bodies (development districts, etc.) on its board. Clearly, local economic development groups and chambers of commerce need to be included on the boards because so much board activity involves economic development. Nonprofit organizations should also have seats, because board decisions affect their interests. For example, local Optimist Clubs, whose purpose is to serve local youth, should have voices in regard to decisions affecting parks and recreation. Dodge's "intercommunity governance network" includes all organized groups in the region. But both Central South Dakota and District III need to give these other organizations more than voices. They need to be given votes to get their full participation. If these organizations obtain partial ownership of the COG's decisions, they may willingly go back to their groups to generate public support for the decisions taken by the COG and later by their local governments.

This inclusion would contribute to the legitimacy of COG decisions, to the legitimacy of local government decisions and ultimately to citizen satisfaction with their governments. Wallis (1994a: 448) says that if a regional governance structure is perceived as legitimate, it is more likely to be granted the capacity to develop and carry out its decisions or to implement its vision.

Wallis's (1994a) second phase deals with the capacity to carry out decisions. As suggested above, if they see decisions as legitimate, taxpayers will be willing to provide the resources necessary to implement the decisions. However, Wallis is not proposing governmental expansion. His second phase does not mean that government will implement the vision. It means that the network created to develop the vision in the first phase will also implement it. An example is NECOG's solution to the internet problem. Neither NECOG nor the local governments had the capacity to solve this problem. However, NECOG, along with its local governments, power companies, schools and others, combined, had that capacity. For this one project, NECOG created Dodge's SIGNET, a Strategic Intercommunity Governance Network.

A leadership problem still exists for these reforms. Each of the potential leaders suggested above, the governor, the legislature, the COG executive directors, and local officials, can provide some leadership. But, no one source of leadership is sufficient by itself. It will take a cooperative effort by all of these leaders if the goal of efficient and effective local government is to be achieved statewide.

South Dakota's COGs are in a unique position to help create such governance. Their executive directors and staffs know most of the political and civic leaders in their regions and can act as the catalysts to bring these groups together to form a network. This would build support not only for their activities but support for the governor and legislature, who are in positions to encourage COG development. Through the political development of COGs, South Dakota could provide more effective and more efficient local government without county consolidation. Through the political development of COGs, the people of South Dakota and their local governments could maintain local control and improve the quality of their lives.

Notes:

1. Counties included: Brookings, Clark, Codington, Deuel, Grant, Hamlin, Kingsbury, Lake, Miner, Moody, Roberts.
2. Counties included: Clay, Lincoln, McCook, Minnehaha, Turner, Union.
3. Counties included: Aurora, Bon Homme, Brule, Charles Mix, Davison, Douglas, Gregory, Hanson, Hutchinson, Jerauld, Lyman, Mellette, Sanborn, Tripp, Yankton.
4. Counties included: Beadle, Brown, Campbell, Day, Edmunds, Faulk, Hand, Marshall, McPherson, Potter, Roberts, Spink, Walworth.
5. Counties included: Haakon, Hughes, Stanley, Jones, Sully, Hyde.
6. Counties included: Bennett, Butte, Custer, Fall River, Harding, Lawrence, Meade, Pennington.

References:

Advisory Commission on Intergovernmental Relations. 1973. *Regional Decision Making: New Strategies for Substate Districts*. Washington, D.C.: Advisory Commission on Intergovernmental Relations.

Berman, David R. 1993. *State and Local Politics*. Madison WI: Brown and Benchmark, Publishers.

Black Hills Council of Local Governments. 1997. "Special Report: 25th Anniversary, 1972-1997."

Dodge, William R. 1992. "Strategic Intercommunity Governance Networks: 'Signets' of Economic Competitiveness in the 1990s," *National Civic Review* 81: 403-417.

Elazar, Daniel. 1966. *American Federalism: A View from the States*. New York: Thomas Y. Crowell.

Henderson, Lenneal J. 1990. "Metropolitan Governance: Citizen Participation in the Urban Federation," *National Civic Review* 80: 105-117.

Kadlecek, James M. 1997. "Cooperation Among Local Governments," *National Civic Review* 86:175.

Profile: South Dakota's Planning and Development Districts. 1994.

Wallis, Allan D. (1994a) "Inventing Regionalism: A Two-Phase Approach," *National Civic Review* 83: 447-468.

Wallis, Allan D. (1994b) "Inventing Regionalism: The First Two Waves," *National Civic Review* 83:159-175.

Wallis, Allan D. (1994c) "The Third Wave: Current Trends in regional Governance," *National Civic Review* 83: 290-310.

Wikstrom, Nelson. 1977. *Councils of Governments: A Study of Political Incrementalism*. Chicago: Nelson Hall.

Discussion Questions:

1. How do you feel about consolidation?

2. How do you feel about government in general?

3. There are many kinds of networks. In your opinion, which kinds are most helpful in maintaining and strengthening community? Why? Which kinds are least helpful? Why?

4. Is enough leadership available on the local and state levels for the COG concept to be effective? If not, how might that leadership be developed?

5. What might South Dakota's cultural diversity have to do with the success or failure of the COG concept?

The Real Wealth of Rural Communities: Changing the Direction of Rural Development

Meredith Redlin

Our rural communities, from all information available, are in trouble. According to the 2000 Census, 15 of the 20 poorest counties in the United States are rural Midwestern counties; the two poorest are agriculturally-based, predominantly white family farm counties in Nebraska. Running close behind are two counties in South Dakota. While in some areas, individual rural incomes have increased, most median rural household incomes have continued to decline over the past four decades. Some of this decline is due to small farm erosion; some is also due to the change in rural small town job structures from independent entrepreneurial business to minimum wage employment in the service sector. Concurrently, there is an increasing gap in most rural communities between wealthy individuals and growing poor populations. While the median wage has lowered, there is also a small rural population that is wealthier than ever. This gap is destabilizing rural quality of life, rural community organizations and rural social institutions. Therefore, the current problems of rural America are not solely those of individuals, but those of communities.

Rural workers are, on average, consistently lower paid than their urban counterparts, sometimes by as much as 30% to 40%. There is widespread and chronic rural unemployment, despite a growth in overall jobs. There is also ongoing deterioration of rural roads, housing, and funding for rural medical and education services. Lack of close access to services creates rural isolation, especially for the elderly. And there is continuing out-migration, almost always of the populations which have most to contribute to the future of our communities, rural youth.

Some of these problems have been noted and studied over the past four decades, and many attempts have been made to address them. In particular, people in rural communities are very familiar with the repeated call for "economic development." Indeed, "economic development" has become the catch phrase for all kinds of political campaigns at the national, state and local level since the 1980s. Unfortunately, however, most attempts at "economic development" in the Midwestern region have been unsuccessful.

Dr. Cornelia Flora, head of the North Central Region Center for Rural Development in Ames, Iowa, argues that these efforts have not been very successful because they have the wrong objectives. In her studies, she has shown that in addition to economic development, rural areas and regions also need more comprehensive community development.

According to Flora, rural community development focuses on finding ways to sustain human, social and natural communities. She argues that three steps are needed to assist our ailing small towns. First, we need to ensure that rural community development takes into consideration all forms of community resources, not merely those which are economic or those that promise unsustainable financial return. Second, we need to ensure that rural community development exists in a policy climate which supports its objectives. Last, any future rural community development must include a clear-headed examination of the traditional economic base of agriculture, considering both its sustainability and its profitability for the community as a whole rather than for select individuals.

These steps require focusing on the rural community, rather than on the rural economy, and inevitably changes some priorities from those of past development efforts. In this approach, capital growth is still the objective of development, but capital growth is no longer simply equated with economic outcomes (Flora, 2001, Welsh and Lyson, 2002). Many rural sociologists now talk about community development in relation to four forms of capital, or wealth, in any community: human, natural, social and financial, or built.

Human capital is the people in the community and their combined skills and talents (Flora, 2001). Developing human capital is a matter of identifying and expanding on people's knowledge and abilities (Flora, 2001; Kretzman and McKnight 2002). Social capital is relationships in the community, particularly those based in civic and volunteer networks (Flora 2001; Putnam 2000). To increase this form of wealth, development planning should include processes which strengthen the ties between community members in existing and new networks. Natural capital is natural resources, such as soil, mining and timber. While it is not always possible to increase natural capital—these resources are most often harvested or extracted—the emphasis in community development (as opposed to mere economic development) is to ensure the sustainability of these resources. That is, development of natural resources must include plans for long-term productivity, and for the least cost to the community for environmental damage and/or clean-up. Flora contends that all of these kinds of capital, or community wealth, are integral to this new approach to comprehensive community development.

In short, community development is more than realizing financial return. It also involves ensuring population stability, increasing civic activity, and improving the overall quality of life of the community. Therefore, even if money is made by an industry in a rural area, it may not be considered to be a successful venture until it also uses and expands the capabilities of the local workforce, participates in and supports community organizations, and follows reasonable environmental practices.

For example, in South Dakota there is now a strong emphasis on the expansion of confinement dairies as a way of improving economies in rural areas. This attention to large-scale, nonsustainable agribusiness is a traditional form of economic development. The focus is on increasing the numbers of jobs and on increasing the value of buildings and operations—all traditional measures of financial and built capital. On paper, the amount of money spent on constructing these ventures and the proposed number of jobs included seem very promising. In reality, however, we have many examples from throughout the nation to show that confinement dairies have not been successful for rural communities in practice.

In California, large dairies have been in existence for many years. We can look at outcomes there and see if large dairies have not only made money (increased financial or built capital), but if they have increased jobs and job skills in the work force (human capital), if they have increased social networks and civic life in the communities where they are located (social capital), and if these operations have resulted in additional costs to the community for environmental management or clean-up (a decrease in natural capital).

When considering not just financial return but also human, social and environmental costs, the results have not been good. In fact, these large California dairies have demonstrated disturbing trends. First, they have often failed financially, because the milk market is saturated and more supply drives prices down even further. Second, while confinement dairies do bring in a number of jobs, they rarely match projections. Some of this discrepancy is due to the time required to bring a dairy confinement operation to full operating level. That is, the dairy may fail before it reaches its projected herd size and production capacity. Additionally, advances in technology and/or management systems have made some promised positions obsolete. While a small number of upper and middle management jobs are created by the new large dairies, the majority of the jobs are minimum-wage, low-skilled positions which are generally not full-time. Therefore, the jobs created have only minimal appeal to the local workforce. Skilled local workers, or those desiring to be so, continue to move elsewhere for good jobs. This out-migration further depletes human capital in the area, which limits possibilities for other kinds of development, such as high technology or manufacturing operations, which require a more skilled workforce.

The dairy contribution to community social capital is also minimal. With a mostly non-local workforce, and often absent owners, these dairy developments are not a significant part of the community. They do not participate as much in activities or community support for schools as local businesses have historically done in rural towns. Further, dairy developments are often brought to the community with promises of little or no tax burden for the business. Therefore, dairies as economic development end up contributing less to the overall economic base than other local agriculture or small business. Furthermore, the addition of a number of low-wage, part-time jobs to the community can increase public costs for social support, medical assistance, housing and road upkeep.

Natural capital for these operations has also been adversely affected. The cost of environmental cleanup of large lagoons or disposal of the large amounts of waste produced in a confinement dairy extends far into the future. Negative environmental impacts, the escalating financial and human costs of increasing agricultural runoff, and water quality deterioration are of growing concern to both urban and rural Americans. These costs are generational, and must be reduced if there is to be a viable future for rural communities.

Overall, the impact of agribusiness development in rural areas like those in California has been negative for communities regardless of the financial balance sheet. Historically, rural communities survived by maintaining "local dollar" circulation. Money earned in the community by workers or owners stayed in the community. But in recent times, "economic development" has come to mean outside investment, which in turn has meant drawing money *out* of rural communities rather than putting money—or good jobs, or cooperative social networks, or environmental safeguards and investments—in.

This example of dairy development demonstrates the importance of using a community, rather than a merely economic, development approach. Rural communities are better off not depending on the "kindness of strangers" for economic investment and support. A better alternative is concentrating on lessening the long-term costs of human, social and natural capital for the community as a whole.

So why don't rural communities just start putting community development plans in place? Unfortunately, it's not that simple, because any form of development and planning depends on policy. Federal rural policy concerning development has been called a "mess"—and worse—as shown in the title and content of the recent book *The Failure of Rural Policy* by William P. Browne (2002). According to Browne, the most common problems of rural policy are:

1) Seeing rural policy as the same as agricultural policy, which doesn't serve the whole rural population, instead forwarding economic development initiatives which provides supports to agribusiness; and

2) Forcing a separation of "urban," "suburban," and "rural" into separate places that don't share the same interests.

These are problems because of some simple demographic facts. First, farmers constitute less than 10% of the total rural population in the United States. Directing a majority of policy efforts at only 10% of any population group simply does not work, whether that population is urban or rural. Also, much of the federal money making its way into local agricultural economies is connected, directly or indirectly, to agricultural development like the dairies discussed above and/or to subsidization. While farmers individually receive subsidies, the largest share goes to large agribusiness interests.

For rural sociologists and others interested in community development planning, the question is not whether or not subsidies should exist. The question is: who is getting the money and where does it go? This matters, because who receives the money affects patterns of local community investment and that all important "local dollar" turnover. If subsidy dollars are going to non-local entities, they are simply a drain of money from the area, and not good community development. If our policy does not identify who is receiving subsidies and supports and where that money ends up, it is a bad policy.

Second, in today's globalized economy, it is almost impossible to consistently distinguish between the interests of rural, suburban and urban populations. Consequently, it is important to think about policies which promote cooperative and complementary growth across areas. Rural advocates pursuing policy for non-farm populations have never proven particularly effective. There have been a number of presidential committees on rural affairs, an equal number of national forums on rural poverty, education, and/or medical care, and numerous single issue groups, such as environmental interests. Yet, none of these has been able to contribute to an overall effective rural policy to supplant that of agriculturally-focused policy. One key problem has been that non-farm initiatives, such as environmental concerns, have been seen as competing with more established farm initiatives for a piece of the federal pie. There has never been an effective and comprehensive rural policy, but instead an ongoing competition within and between farm groups, labor groups, environmental groups, poverty advocates, and so on. As a result, rural communities often end up with self-serving projects, fighting one another for state and federal attention, and undermining their collective needs.

However, grassroots efforts are emerging to challenge that single interest focus. A report of the Rural Policy Forum, which was held in North Dakota in 2002, reflects the importance of a rural policy which complements but is distinct from farm policy. The report's survey discussion emphasizes the need for a New Social Contract "at the heart of all rural policy, if rural communities are expected to survive" (2002:1). This contract, according to the report, should include the following points of agreement that communities can use to move away from special interest policies:

1) Agree that rural is more than agriculture, and so should rural policy be.

2) Agree that the vitality of the country resides in the complex interdependence of rural, suburban, and urban communities; and

3) Agree that innovations and solutions for any area should be derived from local constituents.

As can be seen in these points, the focus on comprehensive rural policy does not preclude input from local community members that addresses their particular interests. Rather, it demands it in order to be effective. The report states this specifically: "Effective policy can only be created with rural stakeholder input—local innovators, local and regional leaders, and diverse rural communities, both ethnically and economically" (2002:3).

This kind of approach creates policy which reflects the goals and objectives of community development, rather than merely those of economic development. Policy that focuses on specific populations, such as rural youth and ethnically or racially diverse groups, specific processes (locally-based objectives) and specific goals (shared interest initiatives for rural, urban and suburban populations) will expedite rural community development.

My discussion of rural policy is not intended to downplay the importance of agriculture to both the rural economy and the rural community. I agree with Osha Gray Davidson when he says that all planning and development of rural areas must include agriculture (1996). But the question is: which form of agriculture is most beneficial for broader rural community viability and success?

A very famous study in the rural sociology on this topic was completed in the late 1940s. The study *As You Sow . . .* was conducted by Walter Goldschmidt, and its conclusions have become known as the "Goldschmidt Hypothesis." Briefly stated, this study contended that the most vibrant rural communities are those with strong and secure family farms.

The original study focused on Arvin and Dinuba—two rural towns in the San Joaquin Valley of California. They were comparable in size, and both were dependent on agricultural economies. Their difference lay in the form of agriculture which surrounded them. While California has never been renowned for its family farm traditions, there are some successful pockets of multi-generational family farms throughout California history. Dinuba was situated in one of these pockets at the time of the study. Arvin was situated nearby, but had a predominantly corporate large-farm base.

Goldschmidt's findings are well-known: The community that was surrounded and dependent on small to mid-sized family farms was the most successful community. That is, Dinuba had more social capital in the form of higher civic participation and more community-based social organizations and volunteerism. Dinuba had more human capital in the form of better schools, a stable population, and a non-transitory workforce for both agriculture and related industries. Dinuba had more natural capital, having better soil conservation and less water loss in its production processes. And Dinuba had less economic stratification; the majority of the population in the community and in the surrounding area was middle-class, with only a small portion representing extremes of either poverty or wealth.

By contrast, Arvin rated lower on all measures. Economic stratification was clearly present in the community, and the workforce was, of necessity, seasonal and transitory. Consequently, community social organizations and schools lacked consistent participation and funding. To offset the costs of labor, agricultural operations relied much more heavily on chemical additives and expanding use of machinery, depleting water and soil resources at a more rapid rate.

Therefore, the Goldschmidt Hypothesis concludes, for rural communities to survive, they must be surrounded by an agricultural tradition which limits the scale of agriculture. The family farm tradition is not restricted in its benefits to the farmers themselves, but also contributes to and depends upon the sustainability of rural communities.

Goldschmidt's findings in this study were controversial when they first came out, arguing against the ongoing trends of the production revolution of the 1940s and 1950s. Yet, they have been reexamined and replicated many times with the same results (for example, Davidson 1996). These findings still show that small and mid-sized family farms best promote rural community health. In fact, studies show that the mid-sized family farm is integral to the retention and success of rural small towns. Admittedly, the definition of what constitutes a "mid-sized" or "small" farm is regionally specific and varies with the commodity grown and with cultivation methods. However, in general, these terms refer to the amount of land that can be farmed by family members alone. For example, when referring to dry-land production of grains in the short-grass prairies of Montana, North Dakota and South Dakota, a mid-sized farm will vary in definition between 1500 and 2000 acres. For more intensive operations, such as irrigation or organics, the amount of land is reduced.

All sizes of agricultural operations have been enduring economic trials for some time. However, the numbers of very small hobby farms and very large super-farms are increasing, while the mid-sized family farm is gradually disappearing from the landscape. Given the evidence of the Goldschmidt study, the elimination of this agricultural form is of great concern to rural sociologists and other community developers. The impact on small towns of the transition to super-farms is great. The best example of that impact is to look at Dinuba today, as the town has been absorbed into the production revolution model during the 1960s. What was an exemplary rural community is now identical to its contrasting community of Arvin. The most recent studies of Dinuba show that there are no mid-sized farms left in the area. Dinuba now no longer has the capital resources it once had. Civic and social participation have evaporated and population levels vary drastically, due to seasonal labor migration. The community infrastructure—roads and services—has deteriorated, resulting in extensive damage in 1998 due to both flooding and drought. Median household incomes have dropped, and the percentage of the population considered to be middle class has decreased. The move to large corporate farms has completely changed the community of Dinuba.

So is Dinuba a clear failure? Not for financial and built capital—agriculture production and the value of goods in the area have more than tripled in that same time. By all other measures, however, Dinuba is a clear failure. The economy may have grown, but the community has diminished. As Cornelia Flora said about the Farm Crisis of the 1980s: "Agriculture is not the problem. Agriculture is doing just fine. It is the people who are having the problems" (1996:13). This comment remains an appropriate description of the ongoing problems in rural communities today. The emphasis on large-scale agribusiness development makes money for individuals, succeeding as an industry. However, that same emphasis deprives rural communities of the capital and support they require to survive. Agribusiness can survive without the rural community, but the rural community cannot survive agribusiness.

Here in South Dakota, we, too, face the mounting problems which are the result of the loss of all forms of capital in our rural areas. The report *Swept Away: Chronic hardship and fresh promise on the rural Great Plains* (Bailey and Preston 2003) provides data which reflects these problems:

• The agriculturally-based counties of South Dakota are the poorest in the region.

• Rural farm counties in South Dakota have poverty rates of 18%, compared with 9% in metro counties in the state.

- South Dakota rates 49th in average income in the United States.
- South Dakota metro counties have averaged $26,557, while rural counties in the state have averaged $20,564—a $6000 difference.

In this same period, South Dakota has had one of the highest rates of job growth in the region, primarily due to service sector increases. Bailey and Preston note: "Combining high job growth with low income and high poverty rates would suggest that South Dakota's rural farm counties are home to an expanding number of low-wage jobs" (2003:35). The growth in jobs in rural areas reflects a worrisome trend for those interested in community, rather than in merely economic, development. While wage and salary jobs and non-farm proprietor jobs have increased, continuing poverty and declining annual income rates indicate that those increases are not sustaining our communities.

Additionally, there are disturbing trends in South Dakota concerning the numbers of mid-sized family farms. The only job rate which continues to drop is that of farm proprietor. The sustaining strength of the surrounding rural population that is key for successful rural communities is being lost.

There are no simple solutions to the complex and tenacious problems in rural America. In fact, given how longstanding, regionally specific and complicated these problems are, it is important that individual communities develop their own new processes, social forms and solutions. This represents the true strength of the community development approach, and its biggest challenge. It requires the involvement of all rural people, not just outside investors and state officials. It must include strategies for encouraging our youth and for convincing them that we can build a future that matters. And it must provide us with the opportunity to grow and change. It must be based on our own involvement in our rural communities (social capital). It must restore our family farm production systems and protect our landscape and natural resources (natural capital). It must be based on our own investment in our rural communities (financial capital). And last, it must encompass our growing understandings of the future of rural life (human capital). This positive change must focus on all of our wealth.

References:

Bailey, Jon and Kim Preston. 2003. *Swept Away: Chronic hardship and fresh promise on the rural Great Plains.* Available through the Center for Rural Affairs, Lyons, NE.

Browne. William P. 2001. *The Failure of National Rural Policy: Institutions and Interests.* Washington, D.C.: Georgetown University Press.

Davidson, Osha Gray. 1996. *Broken Heartland: The Rise of America's Rural Ghetto.* Iowa City: University of Iowa Press.

Flora, Cornelia. 2001. "Introduction." In *Interactions between Agroecosystems and Rural Communities.* Cornelia Flora, ed. New York: CRC Press.

Kretzman, John P. and John L. McKnight. 1993. *Building Communities from the Inside out: A path toward finding and mobilizing a community's assets.* Chicago: ACTA publications.

Putnam, Robert D. 2000. *Bowling Alone: The Collapse and Revival of American Community.* New York: Simon and Schuster.

Welsh, Rick and Thomas Lyson. 2002. *Anti-Corporate Farming Laws, the "Goldschmidt Hypothesis' and Rural Community Welfare.* Available at http://www.i300.org

Discussion Questions:

1. Social capital in any community is usually identified through the number of social organizations present and the number of people who are members. How many social organizations are there in your community? How many people participate in them? Is there a way that you can think of to grow community participation? Are there needs in the community that these organizations can be mobilized to address?

2. Communities' needs can change with their populations. Has the population in your community changed in the last ten years? How? What needs does your community face due to these population changes? How can these needs be addressed?

3. Development often requires building on and expanding the untapped skills of community members. What programs exist in your community to educate young adults? What programs exist in your community to educate working parents or seniors? How can increasing the educational offerings in a community help with building non-financial capital?

4. While there are multiple capitals involved, community development occurs in the context of economic transition and change. What are the primary economic concerns of your community? If business development is key, what structures are in place to develop and encourage additional entrepreneurial efforts? If environmental conservation and protection are key, what steps are community members taking to work with industry to ensure equitable outcomes and a safe environment?

Deeply Rooted in Their Place: Creating a Curriculum that Strengthens Communities

Larry Rogers

Where is this place I live? What is to be learned here about my own life, about the action of desire, about the lives of all of us, living or dead, on this planet? Maybe only the commonest least likely of places will ever permit us inside that question (Holm, 1996, p. 8).

The future of rural America is a subject that concerns most of us who live in the Great Plains. America's originally rural nature—once the dominant aspect of American life—has been in economic, social, and political decline since at least the second quarter of the nineteenth century. As Richard Hofstadter once observed, "The United States was born in the country and has moved to the city" (Hofstadter, 1955, p. 23). Clearly, demographic change in America has been both rapid and dramatic. When the first American census was taken in 1790, the nation was five percent urban and ninety-five percent rural. By 1920, the United States was three-quarters urban. By the time of the 1970 census, the 1790 figures were reversed, and the country was ninety-five percent urban. The depopulation of the countryside continues.

Harlow Hyde, a Nebraska state budget officer, has observed that most rural communities are no more than one generation away from extinction (Hyde, 1997, p. 42). All that it takes for a community to become a shell of what it once had been is for a single generation's young people to lose hope and move away. Examples abound. Sometimes even the national media notices rural decline. *Newsweek's* Chicago bureau chief, Dirk Johnson, wrote in 2001 about the decline of Bisbee, North Dakota, in "Death of a Small Town," noting that Bisbee no longer had a doctor, a lawyer, a plumber, or a priest. When Robert Johnston, a writer for *Education Week*, profiled Howard, South Dakota's educational efforts in 1997, he aptly titled his piece "Learning to Survive."

You don't have to drive more than an hour from where I live to see how fragile community can be. Drive a bit more than twenty miles west on Highway 34 from Madison, the county seat of Lake County, past Howard, the county seat of Miner County, and you will see a sign for a town called Vilas. The sign says that Vilas has a population of twenty-nine, though that estimate seems extremely high. At first glance, there is not much to suggest that Vilas was once a promising place. But if you look closer, you can see traces of that promise. There are two railroad track beds visible through the grass (most towns were lucky to have one railroad; "inland" towns had none), as well as several hundred feet of curb and sidewalk marking the main street's row of businesses. There are remnants of what once was a stockyard, and, until recently, a largely intact building that was once the Oddfellows Hall—a building large enough to have held several dozen people. (The spot where it stood is now open ground, like the rest of Vilas.) Careful pheasant hunters avoid the many grassed over wells and cisterns throughout the area—signs of the many houses that made up the community. Vilas had a population of five hundred in 1880 and two banks, two grain elevators, a general mercantile, and a pool hall. Its future looked promising. Two years later, Vilas lost its bid for the county seat to Howard, and began to die.

Vilas's decline is like that of other Miner County towns. The county's population has declined from over 7,300 in 1945 to less than 2,600 today. Students from Mary Stanghor's English classes in Howard High School visit Vilas every year to consider its fate as they read Osha Gray Davidson's *Broken Heartland: The Rise of America's Rural Ghetto*. They could just as easily visit and study Carthage, Fedora, Roswell, Argonne, or Canova, Miner County's other towns. These students know, of course, that the problem of decline isn't limited to South Dakota. One of their class projects five years ago was the creation of a videotape using scenes from Howard to match up with Davidson's description of life in Mechanicsville, Iowa, a town about the size of Howard. Davis's words about Mechanicsville and the students' images of Howard mesh well. The regular rumors of consolidating county seats in South Dakota as a solution to governmental expense gives Vilas's fate a special meaning for Howard students, though, since this consolidation would mean moving county offices from Howard to Madison.

America's rural decline has been accompanied by considerable confusion, including definitional confusion. For a long time, "urban" status has been conferred by the federal government on any community whose population exceeds 2,500. In North and South Dakota, such a definition means that all but a few communities are "rural," as are all but a handful of the states' school districts. There are other definitions of rural and urban, of course. One such definition of rural—"areas lying outside the standard metropolitan service area of 50,000 population" (Office of Management and Budget)—establishes the other end of the federal government's rural continuum. Depending on which federal department you consult, a rural community is larger than 2,500 people but smaller than 50,000.

This range of definition complicates the difficulty of understanding the changes involved. As Director of the Annenberg Rural Challenge Paul Nachtigal once observed, the rural population is too broad and diverse for a single definition of it to serve as the basis for creating public policy or designing school improvement strategies. How large can a community be and still be considered rural? According to Nachtigal, "it depends" (Nachtigal, 1982, p. 269). Or, as he put it in several conversations with members of the Annenberg Rural Challenge, you're rural if you think you're rural. Whatever definition you choose, South Dakota remains what the Rural School and Community Trust calls

> one of the most rural states: percentages of students in rural schools, schools in rural areas, and students attending rural schools are in the

top three nationally. Fifty percent of every state dollar goes to rural schools (the third highest in the country. Poverty is very high (rural per pupil property wealth in the third lowest in the country), but other challenges are moderate, except for the percentage of English Language Learners (15th largest in the U.S.)(Rural Trust)

South Dakota's farm economy has gone through a series of ups and downs during most of the last century. Every year there are fewer farms, and the ones that are left are bigger, and often owned by people who live outside the state. Every year the populations of most small towns in this region decline. Because South Dakota State University (SDSU) is a land grant institution, it is committed to "providing a continuing stream of knowledge, technology and art for the enrichment of the state and the surrounding region" (South Dakota State University Quarterly Bulletin, 1997, p. 6), Because SDSU was founded as an agricultural college under the Land Grant College Act, and because its largest college is still the College of Agriculture, it must be especially sensitive to these changes.

I am a faculty member in SDSU's Teacher Education Department. Most of my students come from small towns in South Dakota or Minnesota, and most of them want to return to similar communities to live, work, and contribute. A three-year study within the College of Education and Counseling published in 1997 showed that seventy-five percent of the graduates who go into teaching (which is ninety percent of the College of Education and Counseling's graduates) stay in South Dakota. Very few want to leave South Dakota to teach in urban classrooms. Those who do intend to leave usually envision teaching in urban classrooms in the Midwest. Mostly, though, these graduates hope to teach in rural communities.

Early in the twentieth century, Ellwood Cubberly, an influential proponent of school consolidation, wrote that "the rural school is today in a state of arrested development, burdened by education traditions, lacking in effective supervision, controlled largely by rural people, who, too often, do not realize either their own needs or the possibilities of rural education" (Cubberly, 1914, p. 105). Cubberly's quote reflects a common attitude about rural schools, but let me tell you about the rural educators that

I know in South Dakota.

Howard, in southeast South Dakota, an hour from the university, is a prime example of what is possible when people care about a place and try to help save it. It also is an indicator of how a school's curriculum can be revitalized regardless of its place on the rural/urban continuum. Howard's population is a bit under 1,000. Its K-12 school system has about five hundred students. It is the only town in Miner County that provides a full range of social and economic services. The rest of the county's towns are either ghost towns like Argon and Vilas, or are shrinking rapidly like Canova, whose elementary school, the last in the county outside Howard, closed in 1998. Also, population projections are not encouraging. Miner County has lost two thirds of its population through the years, and its farmers quit the land every year.

Nevertheless, Howard's position is hopeful, partly because it has fashioned the strong beginnings of a curriculum of place for its school system. Rather than wait passively to die, the people in Howard determined how to make the school contribute to the community at the same time that it uses the community as a primary curricular resource.

Educators talk often about using the community as a curricular resource. It is a truism in teacher preparation that such a use is essential. But the textbooks that schools actually use offer mostly a national curriculum. They aim to serve the needs of big-market areas like Texas and California, not local interests. They are generic and come in one size that supposedly fits all. In contrast, Jim Lenz, the principal at Howard in 1995, encouraged his teachers to relate their teaching to the community at least once a month. The best example of what they achieved in the first two years of their work can be seen in their community cash flow project (Rogers, 1997, 2001).

The business teacher at Howard, Randy Parry, used an Iowa State University survey of the buying habits of 100 small Iowa towns in his class. The survey showed that only 51% of the respondents shopped locally. Believing that these findings described the economic life of most rural communities, Parry and his students determined to help their community by studying its cash flow patterns and they applied for a curriculum mini-grant from the Program for Rural School and Community Renewal.

The Program for Rural School and Community Renewal at South Dakota State University gave Parry and his students $600 to design, use, and analyze the results of a survey instrument. The topic was a delicate one, for students sought to ask community members to share, albeit anonymously, their economic situations and choices. Having produced a first draft of a survey with the aid of the Future Business Leaders of America advisory board, the students invited all Miner County business owners to a meeting to discuss their project and submitted the first draft to them for their advice. Given strong community support, and having made necessary revisions, the students mailed surveys to a thousand registered voters in the county. Follow-up calls were made to the recipients encouraging them to complete the surveys and thanking them for their cooperation. About forty percent of the surveys were completed and returned—a return rate that was substantially higher than the national average for research surveys. (This high rate of return probably was due to the repeated personal contacts by students.) The results of the surveys were recorded and evaluated by FBLA members using a computer data base and published in the county newspaper.

Randy Parry and his students then made a number of presentations to the community explaining the results of the survey. They also presented their findings to a 1996 regional conference in Sioux Falls sponsored by SDSU's Program for Rural School and Community Renewal and the University of Nebraska's Schools at the Center project. In 1997 they made presentations to the appropriations committees of both the house and senate of the South Dakota legislature in support of a bill that would have used funds from the governor's trust fund for at-risk youth to meet the needs of rural young people.

The students asked twenty-nine questions, but three were especially important questions:

• What percentage of your disposable income do you spend on the following purchases?

• What percentage of these purchases do you make in Miner County?

• What is your household's disposable income?

A series of follow-up questions sought to identify factors that would encourage respondents to spend locally, and several questions dealt with available and desired financial services. The results demonstrated the interplay between ten purchasing categories (automotive supplies, houseware items, groceries, etc.) and six income categories.

To see how delicate the research process was, notice the income distribution within Miner County. There are a lot of poor people in the county. The subject of their income often is a bit tender. It is not a subject that people talk about publicly. The students' sincerity overcame a good deal of natural reticence.

Income Level	Number of people
$14,000	600
$22,000	450
$37,000	100
$52,000	100
$67,500	30
$90,000	30

The cash flow study seemed to yield results that went beyond increased knowledge about the community and more polished research skills. The total increase in spending in Miner County as measured by sales tax receipts in the year following the study was $2,302,384. Multiplying by the formula usually called the economic spending factor, the financial impact of spending in the county was determined to be $7,137,390, despite the fact that the largest employer in the county laid off 112 workers during that period. Spending as measured by sales tax receipts increased by 27%. Seven million dollars in economic impact is a pretty good return for a $600 investment. Did the study lead to the economic upturn? Not many in Howard, or at SDSU, doubt the connection.

The students were far from done. The study was institutionalized into the life of the business course, and it has been adapted to meet new circumstances. For example, taxable receipts decreased one month out of twelve in 1997. The students engaged in additional study to find out why the receipts decreased and what that decrease meant for the county. The study continues to be a model curricular tool, both for Howard and for other small communities. (Several other communities within the Rural Challenge adapted the approach to meet their own needs.)

Through the project, students in Howard learned how to create a research survey, use a data base, and analyze data, and they learned a good deal about how money moves within a community. As Emily Gatsman, a student, said to the house appropriations committee, the students learned these things by using real information, not the fictitious information provided by standard textbooks aimed at a homogenized national market. They learned these things by using their place as a bridge to the traditional subjects they study. At the same time, the students improved their place by contributing to its knowledge base. They also contributed to an understanding of what a true curriculum of place might look like.

Students in Howard engaged in similarly striking work when they conducted a cancer research project (Rural Challenge, 1999, pp. 136-137). Miner County's cancer rate is high. There is hardly a family that does not have personal knowledge of the disease. So the problem became the focus of a schoolwide project coordinated by Mike Knutson, a social studies teacher. Senior English students researched and wrote essays about cancer types, rates, causes, and treatments. Biology students created research-based visual aids to support the essays and tested water quality throughout the county. Sophomore geography students conducted a survey of Miner County residents and created a detailed map that identified cancer clusters in the county. Freshmen computer science students created a data base based on the survey responses. Algebra II students created line graphs that compared cancer rates in Miner County to rates in surrounding counties. Students in the psychology class studied the psychological effects of cancer on county residents, and business law and economics students studied cancer's economic effects. Journalism students wrote a series of stories that considered the overall effect of cancer in the county. Finally, all of the study's threads were woven together for a Community Cancer Day meeting at which students presented their research findings. The results became part of Howard's community web page. There have been no quick solutions to the problems identified by the students, though moving the town's water supply away from an environmentally contaminated site was a start. Nevertheless, the school's curriculum was connected to a very real local problem by means of the study.

Like the cash flow study, the cancer study became the basis for future study. Each study underscored the importance of using place to understand subject matter. Each underscored the value of subject matter for improving place. Each involved the school in the life of the community. Each project contributed to the simultaneous renewal of school and community.

Howard is not the only community engaged in such work. Clear Lake is a town of around 1,300 halfway up the eastern side of South Dakota. It is situated on the edge of what was once unbroken tallgrass prairie country and is close to one of the two largest remaining expanses of such prairie in the state. In many a school district, such a location would not be reflected in the curriculum. Paul Gruchow, who grew up in southwest Minnesota, not far from Clear Lake, attended such a school:

> Among my science courses I took two full years of biology, but I never learned that the beautiful meadow at the bottom of my family's pasture was remnant virgin prairie. We did not spend, so far as I can remember, a single hour on prairies—the landscape in which we were immersed—in two years of biological study.
>
> I took history courses for years, but I never learned that one of the founders of my town and for decades its leading banker—the man who platted the town and organized its school system, its library, its parks, and its fire department—was also the author of the first comprehensive treatise on Minnesota's prairie botany. I can only imagine now what it might have meant to me—a studious boy with a love of nature—to know that a great scholar of natural history had made a full and satisfying life in my town. . . .
>
> I read, in the course of twelve years of English instruction, many useful and stimulating books, but I never learned that someone who had won a National Book Award for poetry—Robert Bly—was living and working on a farm only thirty miles from my house. Nor did I

suspect that it was possible to write books about our countryside. We read Sir Walter Scott, John Steinbeck, and Robert Frost, but not O. E. Rolvaag or Black Elk, Lois Hudson or Thomas McGrath, Meridel LeSueur or Frederick Manfred. (Gruchow, 1995, p. 133-134).

In Clear Lake, the prairie is important. Ramona Lundberg, the biology teacher at Deuel High School in Clear Lake, regularly uses the prairie as a teaching tool. In addition to learning about the ecosphere, she and her students have established baseline data with which to judge the health of their community's natural setting. Attempts are under way to restore clarity to the lake from which the town gets its name. Similar efforts are under way in Willow Lake, eighty miles to the southwest, and in Selby, in western South Dakota.

It would be good to replicate similar surveys and studies in all South Dakota rural communities. It would be valuable for students to carry out detailed studies of their local environments to understand both how they work and how larger environments work.

Several years ago, those of us who worked with the Program for Rural School and Community Renewal at SDSU made suggestions about place-based minigrant topics that we were willing to fund. We thought that field-based studies of flora and fauna (what was native, what was introduced, what had failed, what had thrived) would be useful bridges between subject matter and place. Similarly, we suggested that natural resource audits of water and soil conditions could increase awareness of resource stewardship issues. We believed that baseline data could be established that could inform subsequent studies and protect the biological health of study areas. Community portraits (photographic, video, and written) could capture the heart and/or heartbreak of small rural communities. Data could be collected about how young people spend their free time and recommendations could be made about facilities and resources to make that time worthwhile. Oral history projects could serve to establish relationships between young people and community elders, as could service learning projects.

Many applicants responded to our suggestions. Over one hundred and thirty minigrants were funded within a two-year period, most having been approved by a board consisting of people from South Dakota State University, the Black Hills Special Services Cooperative, and area schools. More significantly, schools also began to fund their own minigrants to build on the earlier ones.

Some of the mini-grant applications proposed interesting ideas that had not occurred to us. A geometry teacher at Howard had a class study the geometric forms of the school district's bus routes and their mathematical efficiency. As it happened, the superintendent had been a pretty good judge of efficiency, but the exercise made the geometric forms more real and could have contributed to a more efficient set of choices. The creation of an outdoor classroom and botanical study center in Rutland led to a study of the establishment and upkeep of shelter belts. Sioux Valley's survey of child care needs contributed to the creation of a consortium with four other towns to support the search for child care funding. Willow Lake forged an alliance with the American Legion to create a community library and museum, having already created a small but useful wellness center.

Not all of the curriculum initiatives were as spectacular as Howard's, but there were others that were stirring in their own ways. Students in the historiography class at Belle Fourche High School (an interdisciplinary class involving the English, history, and business departments) interviewed almost all of the elderly people in their town and created an oral history of the community. They viewed their project as ongoing—the creation of a community historical archive—and preserved their findings using digital cameras and sophisticated computer publications layout software. They produced a magazine, *On the Banks*, and developed a web page that my social studies methods class visited and will visit again. Like the students at Howard, they presented their findings to a community meeting and have given people in their community a new sense of identity by saving their past.

The first issue of *On the Banks* contained twenty-six accounts describing championship games, homesteading attempts, Franklin D. Roosevelt's impact on Belle Fourche, old-time blacksmithing, law enforcement problems, grasshopper infestations, polio epidemics, hard times, and good times. In each case, the person remembering the past was allowed to retain his or her voice. As a result, student interviewer-editors sometimes faced interesting challenges. I was present in the historiography class on the day that several students edited the recollections of Ray Oliver, full-time blacksmith and part-time police officer, about Belle Fourche's World War I-era floating brothel. (The river is small. So was the brothel.) Mr. Oliver retained his distinctive voice (a combination of his speech cadence, word choices, personal values, and oral style), his recollections were made grammatical, the historical record was enriched by his memories, and the students learned to walk an editorial tightrope.

The science teachers at Belle Fourche Middle School also began an environmental survey of a tract of land beside their school. Between the school and the highway, and covering about five acres of land, is a piece of virgin prairie. In addition to studying it, the students are seeking to save it as a school resource. Admittedly, studying it will change it by intruding on the biosystem in place, but not as comprehensively as building a gas station or fast food restaurant on it would. The students will learn about biology while preserving something that is worth preservation.

Of course, personnel turnover (teachers and administrators) and administrative change can undermine initiatives by taking away the continuity in vision that drives them. *On the Banks* came and went, but several of my former students have initiated similar projects in their own schools, having been inspired by the students at Belle Fourche.

Rutland, the smallest of the communities we worked with, has two businesses, a post office, and a school with around 150 K-12 students. Its residents have resisted consolidation for half a century. Their 1994 multi-year school reunion saw almost a thousand people return to the community. Although selling the choice to my dean took some work, Rutland being so small, we funded a feasibility study for the creation of a student-run convenience store. Such a store was needed to provide a community meeting place and to give students valuable experience in economics, though not all lessons would revolve around economics. The plan was prepared by the business class and received the enthusiastic support of the principal, Allen Dvorak. The feasibility study was favorable and led to a couple of years of study by the business students. The store, which opened in 1998, has lived up to expectations. Students make all of its relevant decisions, including the hiring of an adult store manager. Building on the success of this project, teachers at Rutland continue to explore other dimensions of a place-oriented curriculum. The science teacher has used mini-grant funds to help his students conduct a natural resources audit of the area.

So how does an approach that employs curricular mini-grants achieve critical mass in terms of reform? It does so with quick starts and small successes on doable projects as a means of generating enthusiasm and the will to sustain efforts. In a letter to the director of the Program for Rural School and Community Renewal, Paul Nachtigal asked the big questions:

> Under what conditions do doable projects evolve into permanent changes in the way schooling takes place? How long is mini-grant support needed to keep doable projects going? When does this way of learning become an integral part of the education process? At another level, how many doable projects are necessary to get the whole system operating differently? What does the critical mass look like that results in a different set of community expectations around what schools do and how schooling takes place? What will it take to get genuinely good, genuinely rural places? (Nachtigal, 1997, letter, p. 1)

As usual, Howard's experience answered Nachtigal's questions. Other projects continued to be implemented in Howard, most notably the construction of a greenhouse and the planting of an orchard, both of which allow students to study botany and agriculture while growing a set of cash crops that teach them about economics while lowering produce prices at the local grocery. Also, a forty acres plot behind the school has been designated at a potential prairie study center. Another project envisioned clearing local lakes of silt buildup and using the enriched lake matter as fertilizer in test sites for growth comparison. Ultimately, such a project could lead to the creation of a local business that could make use of what students learn.

Most importantly, using Annenberg Rural Challenge money and in-kind local resources like teacher release time, Howard established a rural resource center within the school, with a half-time director. It became a community meeting place, provided a point of contact between the school and the community, and served as an adjunct to the county museum. Its displays were striking. The Veterans' Day display showed the pictures of over four hundred county residents who served during World War II. It was a powerful lesson on the impact of war on South Dakota, as well as on community values. A display highlighting the history of churches in the county was a testament to both hope and disappointment.

It is worth noting that the continued existence of the rural studies resource room wasn't an automatic or easy thing. It took a full-scale community presence (three hundred people) at a 2000 school board meeting to save the center then. The community maintained the center for another year until financial demands on the school district led to the center's demise. In the meantime, Howard's people created the Miner County Revitalization Organization and used their experience with the PRSCR to gain a ten-year $5,000,000 grant from the Northwest Area Foundation— one that recognizes the importance of a curriculum of place. The members of the Miner County Revitalization project's education committee never gave up hope that they would be able to reopen the center. The impressive Rural Learning Center that opened in July, 2006 is both a continuation of the community's efforts in the 1990s and a first stage in what will be a conference center that will allow rural communities to learn with and from each other. (See the Miner County Revitalization website, http://www. mccr.net/, for a view of the future.)

In all of the examples given, the community and its immediate surroundings have become the lens for seeing subject matter with greater clarity. Students have learned about and through their communities by becoming active participants in their communities and in their learning. Their teachers have given them opportunities to strengthen their communities at the same time that they have made the curriculum more meaningful by rooting it in community. As David Orr has argued, integrating place into education allows teachers, students, and community members to combine intellect with experience, combat overspecialization, provide opportunities to deal with tangible problems, and restore a sense of community (Orr, 1992, pp. 128-130). Those are major gains. Place-based learning also does not subject students to lockstep one-size-fits-all curriculum packages. A teacher in another one of the Rural Challenge programs, the Breadloaf Rural Teachers' Network, said it quite well:

> My teaching style reminds me of the great soups of yesterday: not the packaged kind that calls for premeasured packets of ingredients or processed cans of vegetables, but soups created from abundant, local, and available harvests. On my morning commute, as I drive the twisting roads along the river, I inspect the raw ingredients, those ideas that I think will nourish my students. I teach with what is in 'season' (Donovan, 1998, p. 28).

What will it take to create schools in which teachers can "teach in season"? How can teachers be encouraged to teach with the community in mind? What will it take to translate teacher projects like those the PRSCR and other Rural Challenge partners funded into permanent changes in the ways schools operate?

There is some reason for hope. The spirit of the Rural Challenge lives on in the slightly different form of the Rural School and Community Trust, which functions as a think tank, pressure group, research sponsor, and clearing house for ideas and grant opportunities for rural schools and communities. The Rural Trust's Capacity Building Program helps communities study and plan place-based education. (See www.ruraledu.org.) Former Rural Challenge partners—Foxfire, Breadloaf, the National Writing Project, PACERS from Alabama, the Alaska Rural Systemic Initiative, Nebraska's Schools at the Center Project, and others—continue their work. I hope that their work will be continued in cooperation with the faculty at teachers' colleges, for college faculty members and rural communities share more than students. They share the need to produce teachers who are capable of using their places well, teachers who, in Eric Zencey's words,

> take the trouble to include local content in their courses. Not abstract theories about distant peoples, but concrete realizations about observable communities; not airy generalizations that transcend stu-

dent experience and lie beyond their powers of criticism, but specific conclusions whose skeptical testing they can perform themselves; not social-science hearsay taken on faith, but evidence weighed critically, firsthand: these are the substance of a rooted education (Zencey, 1996, p. 10).

What will it take to produce such teachers?

• It will take the willingness of teacher education faculty to abandon one-size-fits-all approaches that are divorced from the particular places in which their future teachers will live and work. Federal legislation—the No Child Left Behind Act, especially—has increased the pressure to accept standards that are not rooted in the places in which teachers and students live. So have national accreditation standards. Despite these pressures, there is a large and growing educational research literature about the ability of small communities to educate young people effectively. Most of that literature strongly reinforces the belief that small districts do better educational work than large ones.

• It will take the willingness of school boards and administrators to use their places as ways to connect with state content standards rather than use state standards as reasons for disconnecting from the places in which they live. Again, there is a growing body of educational research literature that shows how effective place-based curriculum can be.

• Above all, it will take the willingness of national and state educational officials to recognize how good schooling in small towns can be, and to provide adequate support for that schooling.

There is a poem by Ruth De Long Peterson called "Midwest Town." It is part of a collection called *America Is Not All Traffic Lights*—a title that is rooted in this poem. I think of this poem every time I drive to Howard, Willow Lake, or Clear Lake, or places like them, as part of my work. I think especially of its last lines.

Farther east it wouldn't be on the map —
Too small—but here it rates a dot and name. . . .

America is not all traffic lights
And beehive homes and shops and factories;
No, there are wide green days and starry nights,
And a great pulse beating strong in towns like these
(Peterson, 1976, p. 37).

A great pulse beats strong in Howard, and in towns like it. These towns offer a hope of reversing what Paul Gruchow identifies as rural America's leading problem:

If you're any good, you go somewhere else. You go where good people go. We raise our most capable rural children from the beginning to expect that as soon as possible they will leave and that if they are at all successful, they will never return. We impose upon them, in effect, a kind of homelessness. The work of reviving rural communities will begin when we can imagine a rural future that makes a place for at least some of our best and brightest children, when they are welcome to a home among us (Gruchow, 1994, p. 99-100).

Teachers who root their curriculum in their communities can be a powerful force in imagining the kind of rural future that Gruchow describes. They can help students to know their communities as places to be valued, not just as places to leave.

References:

Cubberly, E. *Rural life and education: A study of the rural school problem as a phase of the rural life problem.* (Boston: Houghton Mifflin, 1914).

Donovan, M. Students teaching: In season at people's academy. *Breadloaf Rural Teacher Network Magazine*, Summer, pp. 24-28 (1998).

Gruchow, P. *Grassroots: The universe of hope.* (St. Paul: Milkweed Editions, 1994).

Harbutt, C. The reopening of the frontier. *The New York Times Magazine*, October 18 (1995).

Hofstadter, R. *The age of reform: From Bryan to F.D.R.* (New York: Vintage Books, 1955).

Holm, Bill. *The heart can be filled anywhere on earth: Minneota, Minnesota.* (St. Paul: Milkweed Editions, 1996).

Hyde. H. Slow death in the great plains. *The Atlantic Monthly*, June, pp. 42-45 (1997).

Johnson, D. Death of a small town. *Newsweek*, September 10, pp. 30-31 (2001).

Johnston, R. Learning to survive. *Education Week*, November 28, pp. 34-38 (1997).

Nachtigal, P. Letter to Michael Johnson, February 10, 1997.

Orr, D. *Earth in mind: On education, environment, and the human prospect.* (Washington, D.C.: Island Press, 1994).

Orr, D. *Ecological literacy: Education and the transition to a postmodern world.* (Albany: State University of New York Press, 1992).

Peterson, R. Midwest town, in A. Fleming, ed., *America is not all traffic lights: Poems of the Midwest.* (Boston: Little, Brown and Company, 1976).

Rogers, L. The future of rural America and the problem of rural education. Sewrey Lecture, South Dakota State University, April (1997).

Rogers, L. Curriculum of place and the problem of rural education, in T. Deering, *Issues in teacher education.* (Dubuque, IA: Kendall-Hunt Publishing Co., 2001).

Rural Challenge Research and Evaluation Program. *Living and learning in rural schools and communities: Lessons from the field.* (Cambridge, MA: Harvard Graduate School of Education, 1999).

Rural School and Community Trust, South Dakota profile (http://www.ruraledu.org/site/c.beJMIZOCIrH/b.1069525/k.A177/South_Dakota.htm).

South Dakota State University. *Bulletin Quarterly*, Vol. 87, No. 2, June (1996).

United States Department of Agriculture, Rural Information Center. What is rural? (http://www.nal.usda.gov/ric/ricpubs/what_is_rural.htm) (2005).

Zencey, E. The rootless professoriate, in Vitek, W. and Jackson, W., eds. *Rooted in the land.* (New Haven: Yale University Press, 1996).

Discussion questions:

1. What is the condition of rural America? In what socioeconomic directions is it headed?

2. What do we teach our children about the future of rural America? What do we teach them about their own futures?

3. How can schools and communities work together to strengthen both curriculum and communities? How can they fashion different answers to questions 1 and 2, above, than usually are given?

Selected Readings on Community and Place

John Miller, Larry Rogers, and Charles L. Woodard

Atherton, Lewis. *Main Street on the Middle Border*. Bloomington: Indiana University Press, 1954.

This is a classic study of Midwestern small town life and culture. It pays special attention to the physical structure of small towns and the places where the action occurs. It emphasizes the aspects of the culture that promote community cohesiveness but also notes the groups that get left out or exist on the margins. Atherton's own childhood experiences of growing up in a small town give special authority to his analysis.

Bellah, Robert N., et al. *The Good Society*. New York: Knopf. 1991.

Building on their earlier volume, *Habits of the Heart*, Bellah and four co-authors focus their attention upon American institutions and how well they facilitate the good society. They issue a call for a deeper understanding of the "moral ecology" that builds healthy institutions and communities while counteracting the excessive individualism that is so prevalent today.

_____. *Habits of the Heart: Individualism and Commitment in American Life*. Berkeley: University of California Press, 1985.

This is an acclaimed and best-selling sociological inquiry based on a massive five-year study of a variety of communities that redirected debate about individualism and social commitment in American life. Taking their title from Tocqueville's phrase referring to the mix of traits defining our national character, the authors ask, "How ought we to live?" and "How do we think about how to live?"

Bender, Thomas. *Community and Social Change in America*. Baltimore: Johns Hopkins University Press, 1978.

This is a brief but insightful historical study of the changing structure and meaning of community in the United States. Rejecting "community-collapse" scenarios, it argues that community continues to thrive despite the transformations wrought by urbanization and industrialization.

Boorstin, Daniel J. *The Americans: The Democratic Experience*. New York: Random House, 1973.

This Pulitzer Prize-winning third volume of a trilogy analyzing the entire course of American history emphasizes technological innovations and their influence on society. A central theme is the breakdown of old communities and the rise of new ones, including "statistical" and "consumption" types.

Boyte, Harry C. *Community is Possible: Repairing America's Roots*. New York: Harper & Row, 1984.

Boyte, a political activist and theorist of community organization and citizen participation, provides a practical handbook for people who want to revitalize their communities. He urges Americans to heed the call of a man he once worked for, Martin Luther King, Jr., to "make democracy real in America," providing specific examples of alternatives and empowerment in the spirit of populism and commonwealth.

Christensen, Karen and David Levinson, eds. *Encyclopedia of Community: From the Village to the Virtual World*. Thousand Oaks, CA: Sage Publications, 2003.

The editors observe in the opening sentence of their introduction (p. xxxi) that "community is . . . a central part of being human." This four-volume, 1800+-page work contains essays by 399 contributors. The contributors explore hundreds of different kinds of community and the ways that they are webbed together by the human drive for connectedness. The fourth volume contains an extensive set of resources about building and maintaining community.

Cook, David M., and Swauger, Craig G. *The Small Town in American Literature.* New York: Harper & Row, 1969.

A wide variety of perspectives on small-town America are represented in this strong collection of short stories by some of America's most celebrated authors.

Daly, Herman E., and John B. Cobb, Jr. *For the Common Good: Redirecting the Economy toward Community, the Environment, and a Sustainable Future.* Boston: Beacon Press, 1994.

Rejecting "mainstream" economics, the authors, one an economist and one a theologian, offer a new economic paradigm that will be friendlier to the environment and more conducive to healthy community. Current growth-oriented policies are not sustainable in the long run, they argue. The real economic base of a community consists of those things that make it an attractive place to live and work, including the quality of the natural environment and the richness of the local culture.

Danbom, David. *Born in the Country: A History of Rural America.* Baltimore, MD: The Johns Hopkins University Press, 1995.

Danbom offers a clear, thoughtful history of agriculture and rural life in the United States. As he says at the end, having made it clear how much effort has been required to sustain farming communities, "the countryside is full of . . . [survivors], and we are all the richer for it (270)."

Davis, Peter. *Hometown: A Portrait of an American Community.* New York: Simon and Schuster, 1982.

Prize-winning filmmaker Davis describes the conflicts and passions of a "typical" American community—Hamilton, Ohio—which also served as the basis for a six-part television series.

Dudley, Joseph Iron Eye. *Choteau Creek: A Sioux Reminiscence.* Lincoln and London: University of Nebraska Press, 1992.

Described by renowned South Dakota author Vine Deloria, Jr. as "a warm, human story of people who live close to the earth and each other, learning and living the way we are intended to do," this affectionately written memoir is both person and place-specific and universal in its implications and its meanings.

Etzioni, Amitai. *The Spirit of Community: The Reinvention of American Society.* New York: Simon and Schuster, 1993.

The United States' leading advocate of community describes troubles afflicting American society, tracing many of them to the impact of excessive individualism and overemphasis on individual rights. He proposes solutions to be found in a renewed and rebalanced social contract that both protects individual rights and serves and protects the needs of society.

Gallagher, Winifred. *The Power of Place: How Our Surroundings Shape Our Thoughts, Emotions, and Actions.* New York: Simon & Schuster, 1993.

Gallagher, an award-winning journalist, draws upon recent research in the environmental and behavioral sciences to illuminate the relationships that exist between people and the places where they live, work, and interact with others.

Greene, Bob. *Once Upon a Town: The Miracle of the North Platte Canteen.* New York: HarperCollins, 2002.

This is the inspiring story by an award-winning journalist of how one community of 12,000 residents in Nebraska joined together during World War II to provide welcoming words, friendship, and baskets of food to thousands of soldiers passing through on troop trains going east and west. Going back to visit the town at the dawn of the twenty-first century, Greene finds the center of town has moved from Main Street to a twenty-four-hour Wal-Mart, whose lot is so full of cars that it is a challenge to find a parking space.

Gruchow, Paul. *Grass Roots: The Universe of Home* (St. Paul, MN: Milkweed Editions, 1995).

Gruchow's marvelous essays deal directly with place and community; e.g., "Discovering One's Own Place," "What the Prairie Teaches Us," and, most importantly, "What We Teach Rural Children."

Haas, Toni and Paul Nachtigal. *Place Value: An Educators' Guide to Good Literature on Rural Lifeways, Environments, and Purposes of Education.* (Washington, D.C.: ERIC Clearinghouse on Rural Education, 1998).

Haas and Nachtigal, co-directors of the much-remembered Annenberg Rural Challenge, provide five bibliographic essays that emphasize how rural America is shaped by its ecology, politics, economic structures, values, and educational arrangements.

Hasselstrom, Linda. *Leaning into the Wind: Women Write from the Heart of the West.* Boston: Mariner Books, 1998.

Hasselstrom, a South Dakota writer and rancher, has gathered prose and poetry from a wide variety of women living in the Great Plains and the West. The voices of the women she includes in the three collections make strong, clear statements about the need for community in the face of distance and separation.

_____. *Woven on the Wind: Women Write about Friendship in the Sagebrush West.* Boston: Houghton Mifflin, 2001.

_____. *Crazy Woman Creek: Women Rewrite the American West.* Boston: Mariner Books, 2004.

Hine, Robert V. *Community on the American Frontier: Separate but Not Alone.* Norman: University of Oklahoma Press, 1980.

Hine describes the huge importance of community formation on the frontier as it pushed westward during the nineteenth century. Community was expressed in multiple ways, including church activities, ball games, barn raisings, and shared work. "Wherever community thrived on the frontier it was framed by a sense of place," Hine writes.

Jackson, Wes. *Becoming Native to This Place*. Counterpoint, 1996.

Jackson is a biologist who has been involved with agricultural experimentation for years at the Land Institute in Matfield Green, Kansas, a model of earth-friendly farming techniques. He applies the idea of place to the subjects of ecological maintenance and agrarian reform in powerful ways.

Keillor, Garrison. *Lake Wobegon Days*. New York: Viking, 1985.

Based on monologues presented on his popular weekly Public Radio program "Prairie Home Companion," Keillor gently satirizes the foibles and anomalies of small-town communities while simultaneously affirming the positive qualities of living in places that are set on a human scale. His deft dissections of various aspects of community life contain insights worth pondering by social scientists and lay people alike.

Kemmis, Daniel. *Community and the Politics of Place*. Norman, OK: University of Oklahoma Press, 1992.

Kemmis, who was mayor of Missoula, Montana, and a Montana legislator, writes clearly about civic engagement and the polarization that undermines it. He has a sense of history as well as a visionary politician's grasp of the details of government. He makes a clear case for the importance of grass-roots involvement in government and directly addresses the building of community in the face of challenging circumstances. His *The Good City* and *The Good Life* (New York: Houghton Mifflin, 1995) carries beyond Montana.

Kloefkorn, William. *Restoring the Burnt Child: A Primer*. Lincoln and London: University of Nebraska Press, 2003.

This is an engaging memoir about a Midwestern boy's evolving attitudes toward the small towns of his childhood combined with looking-back commentaries which are witty and very insightful.

Kunstler, James Howard. *The Geography of Nowhere: The Rise and Decline of America's Man-Made Landscape*. New York: Simon & Schuster, 1993.

The importance of place in community health shines through clearly in this highly readable account of the way in which the Unites States changed from a country marked by Main Streets and coherent communities to one defined by suburban freeways, parking lots, and malls, where every place is like no place in particular. He calls on Americans to reinvent the places where they live and to work to rebuild communities that are life-affirming.

Lasch, Christopher. *The Culture of Narcissism: American Life in an Age of Diminished Expectations*. New York: W.W. Norton, 1978.

Lasch's book gave a name to the decade of the seventies. The narcissistic personality of our time eventually discovers that escaping from traditional taboos and restraints brings no spiritual peace. The author yearns for love, self-restraint, and a new spirit of community that will replace a culture of narcissistic self-absorption.

Ledeen, Michael A. *Tocqueville on American Character*. New York: St. Martin's Press, 2000.

Taking off from great French social commentator Alexis de Tocqueville's incisive comments on the high level of volunteerism and community in early nineteenth-century America, Ledeen wonders whether Americans have fallen into moral decay and religious indifference. A healthy tradition of "collective individualism" is in danger of disintegrating and needs reinvigoration if we are to retain healthy communities.

Lingeman, Richard. *Small Town America: A Narrative History, 1620-The Present*. New York: G. P. Putnam's Sons, 1980.

Evolving notions of community are traced in the history of America's small towns over the course of three and a half centuries. It is a lively discussion of the transformations small towns have undergone by a popular journalist, social historian, and biographer of Sinclair Lewis.

Louv, Richard. *America II*. Los Angeles: J. P. Tarcher, 1983.

Community is revealed in this broad-ranging sketch of fundamental shifts in lifestyles and attitudes between "America I" (big cities, big labor, railroads, public swimming pools, New Deal-style politics, and freestanding single-family homes) and "America II" (rural shopping malls, condominiums, planned communities, private police forces, and high-tech homes and workplaces).

Lynd, Robert S., and Helen Merrell. *Middletown: A Study in American Culture*. New York: Harcourt, Brace & World, 1929.

This classic study of community as manifested in the daily experiences of residents of a "medium-sized" Midwestern urban place (Muncie, Indiana) during the 1920s. It traces the changes that transformed life there during the previous quarter-century. The book's observations and interpretations also shed light on smaller communities, which experienced similar transformations during the period.

Maharidge, Dale. *Denison, Iowa: Searching for the Soul of America Through the Secrets of a Midwest Town* (New York: Free Press, 2005).

The text, accompanied by photographs from the *Washington Post's* Michael Williamson, spotlights the tensions and challenges generated in Midwestern small towns in recent decades as increasing numbers of Latinos move in to take jobs. Denison, a town of 8,000 in west central Iowa, is learning to cope and deal with the profound changes that occur during the process of cultural assimilation and transformation.

Marshall III, Joseph. *The Dance House: Stories From Rosebud*. Santa Fe: Red Crane, 1998.

In a conversational and engaging voice, the author presents a panorama of past and present community life on his South Dakota reservation in this strong collection of essays and short stories.

Martone, Michael. ed. *A Place of Sense: Essays in Search of the Midwest*. Iowa City: University of Iowa Press, 1988.

This is a lively collection of essays about life in farming communities, small towns, and suburbs in America's so-called "heartland."

McNeil, Tom. *Goodnight, Nebraska* (New York: Vintage Books, 1999).

McNeil's book is a novel about the power of a small community to turn around the direction of a young life that has been lived badly. It does not descend into romanticism and it taps into a theme that marks a large number of novels, such as *Plainsong* (New York: Alfred A. Knopf, 1999) and *Eventide* (New York: Alfred A. Knopf, 2004) by Kent Haruf. All see the power of community, even, perhaps especially, in adverse circumstances.

Meyers, Kent. *Witness of Combines* (Minneapolis, MN: University of Minnesota Press, 1998).

Meyers writes a memoir in the form of overlapping essays. The title essay alone explains much about how community is formed and retained on the Plains in its description of neighbors rallying to harvest the crop of someone that not all of them even like. Meyers' point is reinforced by Michael Perry's *Population 485* (PS)(New York: Harper Perennial, 2003), which describes life in New Auburn, Wisconsin. Perry learns about his new community by joining the volunteer fire and rescue squad, a position that allows him to meet his neighbors "one siren at a time." Both books emphasize what social capital looks like in the lives of neighbors who face common challenges.

Meyrowitz, Joshua. *No Sense of Place: The Impact of Electronic Media on Social Behavior*. New York: Oxford University Press, 1965.

Building upon the work of Erving Goffman, Marshall McLuhan, and other social scientists, Meyrowitz demonstrates how place and community have become disconnected by the growing pervasiveness of the modern media. By bringing many different types of people together in the same "place," the electronic media create new social environments that blur many formerly distinct social roles that were attached to particular places.

Miller, John E. *Looking for History on Highway 14*. Pierre, SD: South Dakota State Historical Society Press, 2001.

This historical-journalistic travelogue examines the notion of community from a variety of perspectives, focusing its attention upon fifteen small towns located along Federal Highway 14 in South Dakota and illustrating how historical memory, architecture and monuments, art, stories, and social rituals feed into community.

Momaday, N, Scott. *The Names: A Memoir.* Tucson: University of Arizona Press, 1976.

A richly philosophical exploration of past and present communities and cultures, this poetically evocative memoir by a Pulitzer Prize-winning novelist also dramatizes the importance of place and human relationship to emotional well-being.

Nisbet, Robert A. *The Quest for Community.* New York: Oxford University Press, 1953.

Calling the quest for community a dominant social tendency of the twentieth century, Nisbet traces the forces and dislocations that led to an obsessive concern with community in modern literature, philosophy, and social science as well as in popular thought and culture.

Norris, Kathleen. *Dakota: A Spiritual Geography.* New York: Ticknor and Fields, 1993.

In this widely acclaimed book, the author examines the small South Dakota community where she spent portions of her childhood, meditates on the strengths and weaknesses of such places, and characterizes the outside forces which threaten them.

Oldenburg, Ray. *The Great Good Place: Cafes, Coffee Shops, Community Centers, Beauty Parlors, General Stores, Bars, Hangouts, and How They Get You Through The Day.* New York: Paragon House, 1991.

Emphasizing the importance of place in people's lives, Oldenburg argues that "third places," where people gather for good company and lively conversation, are vital for community quality and democratic politics.

Orr, David. *Earth in Mind: On Education, Environment and the Human Prospect* (Washington, D.C.: Island Press, 1994).

Orr's essays center on the future of rural America. Two of the book's sections—"The Problem of Education" and "Rethinking Education"—were read in the 1990s by the faculty discussion group at SDSU that led eventually to the book you are holding.

Pappano, Laura. *The Connection Gap: Why Americans Feel So Alone*. New Brunswick: Rutgers University Press, 2001.

Evidence for a "connection gap" in the United States can be found in the decline of meaningful interaction, a growing sense of unreality, feelings of loneliness, the appeal of nostalgia, and other factors. Pappano wants people to rebuild community by reconnecting to place, redesigning their residences, reinvigorating family life, cultivating friendship, reviving conversation, keeping technology in its proper place, and strengthening institutional supports.

Pipher, Mary. *The Middle of Everywhere: Helping Refugees Enter the American Community*. Harvest Books, 2003.

Pipher, a family therapist in Lincoln, Nebraska, writes movingly about the need for established Americans to serve as cultural brokers for the refugees who reach this country having experienced war and dislocation. Her book is a hands-on introduction to what it means to build community in a new and challenging place while enlarging our collective definition of community.

Putnam, Robert D. *Bowling Alone: The Collapse and Revival of American Community*, New York: Simon & Schuster, 2000.

Based upon massive quantitative data, Harvard political scientist Putnam attracted considerable public attention with this detailed study of declining participation in social organizations, community groups, recreation clubs, political parties, and, as the title of the book implies, bowling leagues. Interestingly, the two Dakotas rank highest in the kind of "social capital" he hopes to reinvigorate—communal activity and community sharing that make people's lives more pleasurable and meaningful.

Putnam, Robert D., and Lewis M. Feldstein. *Better Together: Restoring the American Community*. New York: Simon & Schuster, 2003.

Following up on his widely-discussed *Bowling Alone*, Putnam focuses here upon a dozen "social-capital success stories," hoping and believing that they are indicators of a revival of social capital in the United States. These stories—including ones about branch libraries in Chicago, a neighborhood group in Boston, and a community church in Lake Forest, California—are meant to inspire and guide readers to get involved in their own communities in ways to improve and revivify them.

Russo, David J. *American Towns: An Interpretive History*. Chicago: Ivan R. Dee, 2001.

This is a wide-ranging interpretive history of small towns that, in addition to chapters on politics, economics, society, and culture, includes one on geography and design. Russo concludes that since the late nineteenth century, people's life experiences in small towns have gradually converged with those of people in cities and suburbs.

Schudson, Michael. *The Good Citizen: A History of American Civic Life*. New York: Free Press, 1998.

In focusing on citizenship and its requirements, Schudson illuminates one of the essential elements of community life. Although Americans are more neighborly and civic-minded than Europeans, they are more spatially divided, being much more likely to own their own homes and to spend considerable sums on improving them. While people in small towns remain connected socially, economically, and politically, the dominant majority of metropolitan dwellers live much more divided lives, attenuating community ties.

Smith, Page. *As a City Upon a Hill: The Town in American History*. Cambridge: MIT Press, 1966.

This general survey of the evolution of small towns from colonial times to the present places town building at the heart of the American historical experience. Smith finds that two types predominated: "colonized towns," settled by relatively homogeneous ethnic and religious groups, and "cumulative towns," which were more diverse and grew rapidly and generally without plan.

Sneve, Virginia Driving Hawk. *Completing the Circle.* Lincoln: University of Nebraska Press, 1993.

Using the central image and metaphor of the quilt, the author of this rich text, South Dakota's National Humanities Medalist, describes and celebrates the strong and creative and purposeful tribal women from whom she has descended, and shares tribal community history and legendry and her own meaningful coming-of-age experiences in the process.

Stein, Maurice. *The Eclipse of Community: An Interpretation of American Studies.* Princeton: Princeton University Press, 1960.

Stein draws on studies by Robert and Helen Lynd, Robert Park, and others to sketch his theory of community development. He then applies that theory to specific case studies, including one of Southern towns, and traces the ways in which urbanization, industrialization, and bureaucratization affect contemporary communities.

Theobald, Paul. *Teaching the Commons: Place, Pride, and the Renewal of Community.* Boulder, CO: Westview Press, 1997.

Theobald's defense of rural schools and rural communities is grounded in both a clear historical vision and in personal experience with rural educational reform. The third section, "Education and the Renewal of Community," gives clear examples of how rural schools can serve to strengthen rural communities.

Vitek, William and Jackson, Wes. *Rooted in the Land: Essays on Community and Place.* New Haven, CT: Yale University Press, 1996.

The thirty essays in this book include pieces by Wendell Berry ("Conserving Communities"), Linda Hasselstrom ("Addicted to Work"), David Orr ("Re-ruralizing Education"), Daniel Kemmis ("Barn Raising"), Cornelia and Jan Flora ("Creating Social Capital"), and two dozen others that deal directly with issues of community building, maintenance, and loss.

Wiebe, Robert H. *The Search for Order, 1877-1920.* New York: Hill and Wang, 1967.

This is a seminal interpretation of the half-century following the Civil War, a period in which individualistic values and practices associated with a small-town, rural agrarian society gave way to new ones attached to an emerging urban, industrial society. Wiebe argues that the United States evolved from a nation of isolated "island communities" in the years right after the Civil War to òne of a more integrated set of urban places after the turn of the century.

Wuthnow, Robert. *Sharing the Journey: Support Groups and America's New Quest for Community.* New York: Free Press, 1994.

Refuting the thesis that the United States is becoming an alienated society, this leading advocate of community argues that the rapid expansion of the support group movement reveals another side of our behavior. Drawing upon the results of a national research project on small groups and spirituality, Wuthnow's description of groups ranging from AA to prayer fellowships to abuse prevention provides evidence of new dimensions of self and community in America.

The Contributors

Darla Bielfeldt takes inspiration from the landscape, textures, and oral stories of the American Midwest. Her musical training has fostered her interest in the interplay of words with sound and timing. Bielfeldt completed her M.A. in creative writing from Iowa State University, studying with Mary Swander, Neil Bower, Fern Kupler, and Stephen Pett. At Iowa State, Bielfeldt also studied musical composition. She has taught English at GrandView College, Iowa State, and South Dakota State University. She also frequently works as a collaborative pianist, and is currently the accompanist for the Heartland Opera Troupe.

Dennis Bielfeldt is Professor of Philosophy and Religion at South Dakota State University, an ordained Lutheran minister, and a musician who performs throughout the area. His Ph.D. in Religion is from the University of Iowa. He has published a book, *Freiheit und Liebe bei Martin Luther*, and numerous scholarly articles and reviews, and he is a frequent presenter and featured speaker at conferences and seminars. He is also president of Den-Wil, Inc., Brookings.

Doug Cockrell was born in Huron, South Dakota, and graduated from Redfield High School, Redfield, South Dakota, in 1971. He received a B.A. in English from South Dakota State University in 1975, and he has also done post-graduate work in creative writing. He has had poems published in numerous magazines, journals, and anthologies, and his book of poems entitled *A Strange Descending*, which was recently the subject of a feature story in *The Rapid City Journal*, was published in 1992. He has three children, Laura, Robert and Christine, and he now lives in Huron, and continues to write.

Nels H. Granholm was born June 17, 1941 (Bunker Hill Day) in Boston at Massachusetts General Hospital. He graduated with a B.A. degree in Biology from the University of Massachusetts, Amherst, an M.A. in 1964, and completed a Ph.D. in Developmental Biology at Iowa State University in 1968. While in Ames, Nels met Dee Reyelts of Britton, South Dakota, and they were married on May 8, 1965, in Ames. Subsequently, Dee, Nels, and three sons David, John, and Daniel have been living and enjoying life (most of the time) in and around Brookings, Mount Desert Island, Maine, and Macclesfield, England. Nels has been teaching biology, honors courses, and global studies courses at SDSU for 37 years (about 30% of the existence of SDSU). His essay on biological community is a reflection of his deep and profound appreciation for nature and the indispensable human requirement (sine qua non) to stay connected to the land.

Ruth Harper is Professor of Counseling and Human Resource Development at South Dakota State University, where she coordinates the Student Affairs track. Her degrees were earned at Cornell College, the University of Wisconsin-Oshkosh, and Kansas State University. Ruth believes that counseling, at its best, helps people "stop conspiring in their own diminishment and start living by their own best lights" (Parker Palmer). She is co-author of *Assisting Students with Disabilities: A Handbook for School Counselors* (Corwin Press, 1999; 2007) and currently edits the *Counseling Today* resource review (an American Counseling Association publication). Ruth is particularly interested in college student development, career counseling, American Indian college students, and students with disabilities. She loves poetry and writes a bit of it on occasion. Ruth is married to Larry Rogers. They have three daughters who sometimes appear to be amazing young adults.

Mary Alice Haug grew up on a farm in central South Dakota. She has taught English at South Dakota State University for nearly 30 years, focusing on literature from the Great Plains region. She has been published in *Crazy Woman Creek, One House, Many Skies, South Dakota Magazine,* and *On the Homefront: South Dakota Stories,* and had an essay accepted by Radio Works.

William Kloefkorn is Professor Emeritus at Nebraska Wesleyan University in Lincoln and the Poet Laureate of Nebraska. He has been published in a wide variety of literary journals and anthologies, and he is the author of numerous books of poems, including *Alvin Turner as Farmer, ludi jr, Treehouse: New and Selected Poems, Drinking the Tin Cup Dry,* and *Sunrise, Dayglow, Sunset, Moon.* His prose includes two memoirs, *This Death by Drowning* and *Restoring the Burnt Child: A Primer,* both from the University of Nebraska Press.

Ted Kooser recently served two terms as Poet Laureate of the United States. He has authored eleven volumes of poetry and several prose volumes, and his book entitled *Delights and Shadows* was awarded the Pulitzer Prize for Poetry in 2005. He has also been awarded the Society of Midland Authors Prize, the Pushcart Prize, the Stanley Kunitz Prize, and the James Boatwright Prize. A retired insurance company executive, he is a professor of English at the University of Nebraska. He lives on an acreage near Garland, Nebraska, with his wife Kathleen.

Elden Lawrence is a member of the Sisseton Wahpeton Oyate in South Dakota. One of 10 children, he attended the Flandreau Indian School briefly, and then enlisted in the United States Army at the age of 17, where he served six years, including a tour of duty in Korea. Having obtained his GED certificate, he then completed an undergraduate degree at Sisseton Wahpeton College, and later he earned a Ph.D. in Rural Sociology from South Dakota State University. Following his graduate work, he served as President of Sisseton Wahpeton College for several years, providing leadership during an especially challenging transitional time for that institution. He also served two terms on the Sisseton Wahpeton Oyate Tribal Council, and one term as Tribal Secretary. He was recently Visiting

Professor of Ethnic Studies, University of Minnesota-Mankato. His publications include a recent book, *The Peace Keepers: Indian Christians and the Dakota Conflict.* Elden and his wife Kim have two children, Derrick and Deborah, and six grandchildren.

MaryJo Benton Lee holds bachelor's and master's degrees in journalism from the University of Maryland-College Park, and a Ph.D. in Sociology, with a minor in Asian Studies, from South Dakota State University. During her 22 years at SDSU she has held a number of positions, both teaching and administrative, most recently that of Diversity Coordinator for the College of Engineering and Coordinator of the SDSU-Flandreau Indian School Success Academy. Her first book was *Ethnicity, Education and Empowerment: How Minority Students in Southwest China Construct Identities.* Her second book was *Ethnicity Matters: How Black, Hispanic, and Indian Students Prepare for and Succeed in College.*

Delmer Lonowski is Professor of Political Science at South Dakota State University. He was trained at the University of Nebraska-Lincoln. He teaches state and local government and brings to his class, and to his article, his experience as the Sherman County representative on the Nebraska Region 26 Council of Governments.

John E. Miller, a writer and historian, taught American History for almost three decades at South Dakota State University. His books include *Looking for History on Highway 14* and *Becoming Laura Ingalls Wilder: The Woman Behind the Legend.* Involved in many humanities programs over the years, he has taken a particular interest in small towns and the enhancement of community and social capital. He is one of the founders of the SDSU Community Group, has served as a Boy Scout scoutmaster, and is actively involved in church activities.

Joe Paddock is an poet, oral historian, and environmental writer. He has been a Humanist in Residence with the American Farm Project, a regional poet for southwest Minnesota, a Poet in Residence with Minnesota Public Radio, and an adjunct faculty member in the Creative Writing Department of the University of Minnesota. He is a founder of the Land Stewardship Project, and is the principal author of the environmental book *Soil and Survival*. He has been involved with the production of more than 20 project books, and is the author of *Keeper of the Wild*, the biography of wilderness preservationist Ernest Oberholtzer. His books of poetry include *Handful of Thunder, Earth Tongues, Boars' Dance* and *A Sort of Honey*. For his poetry, he has received the Lakes and Prairies Award of Milkweed Editions and the Loft-McKnight Award of Distinction. He lives with his writer wife Nancy Paddock in the house he grew up in in Litchfield, Minnesota.

Meredith Redlin is an Associate Professor of Rural Sociology at South Dakota State University, where she specializes in rural community studies. She earned her master's in Interdisciplinary Studies from Hamline University in St. Paul, Minnesota, and her Ph.D. in Sociology from the University of Kentucky in Lexington.

Larry Rogers is Professor of Education at South Dakota State University. His degrees were earned at the University of Nebraska in Lincoln. He has taught high school and college history courses for the Lincoln and Omaha school systems, Nebraska Wesleyan University, Sioux Falls College, and SDSU. He has taught teacher education courses (especially social studies teaching methods and secondary curriculum) at the University of Sioux Falls and SDSU. Directly related to his essay topic, Larry was associate director of the Program for Rural School and Community Renewal, an affiliate of the Annenberg Rural Challenge, from 1995 until 2000. Larry is married to Ruth Harper and shares three daughters with her. His commitment to the Chicago Cubs is deeply rooted.

Lydia Whirlwind Soldier is a Sicangu Lakota born in Bad Nation on the Rosebud Reservation in South Dakota, and she is an enrolled member of the Rosebud Sioux Tribe. She has a Master's in Education Administration from Penn State University, and she has worked in education for over thirty years. She is also a poet, a non-fiction writer, a business owner, and a recognized craftswoman. In 1994 she received first place at the Northern Plains Tribal Arts Exposition in Sioux Falls, South Dakota. *Memory Songs*, her collection of poems, was published in 1999, and she co-authored *Shaping Survival: Essays by Four American Indian Tribal Women*,which was published in 2001.

Ruby R. Wilson graduated with degrees in German and Geography from South Dakota State University, where she is presently employed in the Archives and Special Collections Department. Her poetry and prose have been published in *Woven on the Wind, Crazy Woman Creek, Arts Alive*, and other publications. She is a native South Dakotan who has lived most of her life in small communities in the state. She now lives on a small acreage near Brookings, South Dakota.